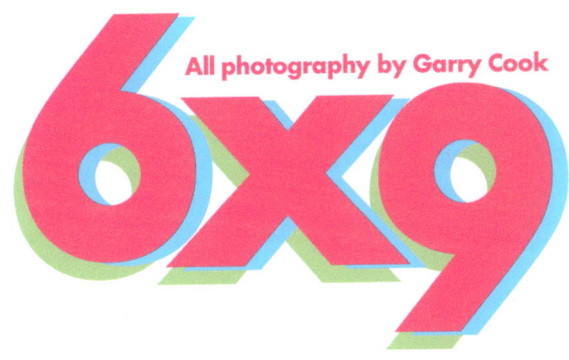

All photography by Garry Cook

ISBN-13: 978-1466301641
ISBN-10: 1466301643

Garry Cook's 6x9

Smoking

Around the time the ban on smoking in public places came into force in England, I visited bingo halls, nightclubs, pubs, shisha cafes and social clubs to document smokers doing something about to become illegal.

I photographed in Manchester, Liverpool, Blackpool and Preston. On the day of the ban – July 1, 2007 – and in the weeks after, I documented smokers as they were forced to go outside for the first time.
All photographs taken in 2007.

Blackpool Glitz

Since 2006 I have travelled to the brash trash glamour and the brightly-lit glitz that forms the heart of Britain's most famous seaside town. I find Blackpool as enthralling and addictive as it is dirty and depressing.

Having worked in Blackpool I am aware of the deprivation which lies behind the Golden Mile. And, as much as it tries not to be, the Promenade feels like deprivation glossed over with fluorescent paint.

I often get criticised for my images of Blackpool but, as with all my photography, I attempt to present what I find. I'm not here to make somewhere look pretty when it quite clearly isn't.

Those promoting the town are on a never-ending quest to drag Blackpool away from its image as a day-time pensioner's paradise and night-time stag-do party town. They are ashamed of this image. I think it should be celebrated.

Without these visitors, the place would have died long ago.
All photographs taken between 2006 and 2010.

God Hates America

A day spent with the Phelps family in Topeka, Kansas State, USA.

The Phelps are the founders and almost exclusive members of the Westboro Baptist Church.

They picket ceremonies, rival churches, local newspapers and funerals, mainly to object against homosexuality and the people who are tolerant of it.
All photographs taken in 2008.

O Little town of Bethlehem

I visited Bethlehem in September 2008. I read the advice from the British Foreign Office, I researched press articles about the region and watched news stories on TV. As far as I was concerned, I was heading into a war zone.

Bethlehem, I'm sure you've heard of it (birthplace of Jesus etc etc) is a small town south of the city of Jerusalem.

It is separated and isolated from the beautiful walled city of Jerusalem by its own unique wall – a monolithic travesty in modern architecture.

Bethlehem is situated in the West Bank, a Palestinian Territory. The area is controlled by the Israel Defence Forces (the Israeli Army).

The wall is a huge concrete eyesore which curves round most of the town.

It is a lesson in how not to deal with a social problem.

On the Palestinian side, the wall has been heavily graffitied. The huge drawings are packed with humour and irony.

And it is this humour which can be seen on the streets of Bethlehem from a people undeniably subjugated yet who remain welcoming (unless you're haggling over the cost of a taxi to Beit Ummar).
All photographs taken in 2008.

Tourism in India

Massive country, massive population, massive poverty.

An outsider's view of India is as clichéd as it is true.

But there is much more to the country. Massive growth in industry, massive growth in tourism.

India still has a long way to go in terms of development (road journeys across the Punjab give me nightmares even now) but there is an increasing opportunity in the country for people to work and earn money.

And from that comes domestic tourism – recreational holidays and day's out for Indian people.

I travelled to Delhi and Agra, across the Punjab and to the Himalayan foothills with Indian families documenting Indian people at play.
All photographs taken in 2009.

Christmas!

December is the season to be jolly. It's also the time we think about those things most important as we approach the birth date of Jesus Christ – shopping, partying and eating.

This series of images documents what Christmas means in modern-day Britain.
All photographs taken in 2009.

Cover image: Taken at Jasper Joffe's Beautiful/Ugly exhibition in 2008.

Come to where the smoking is.

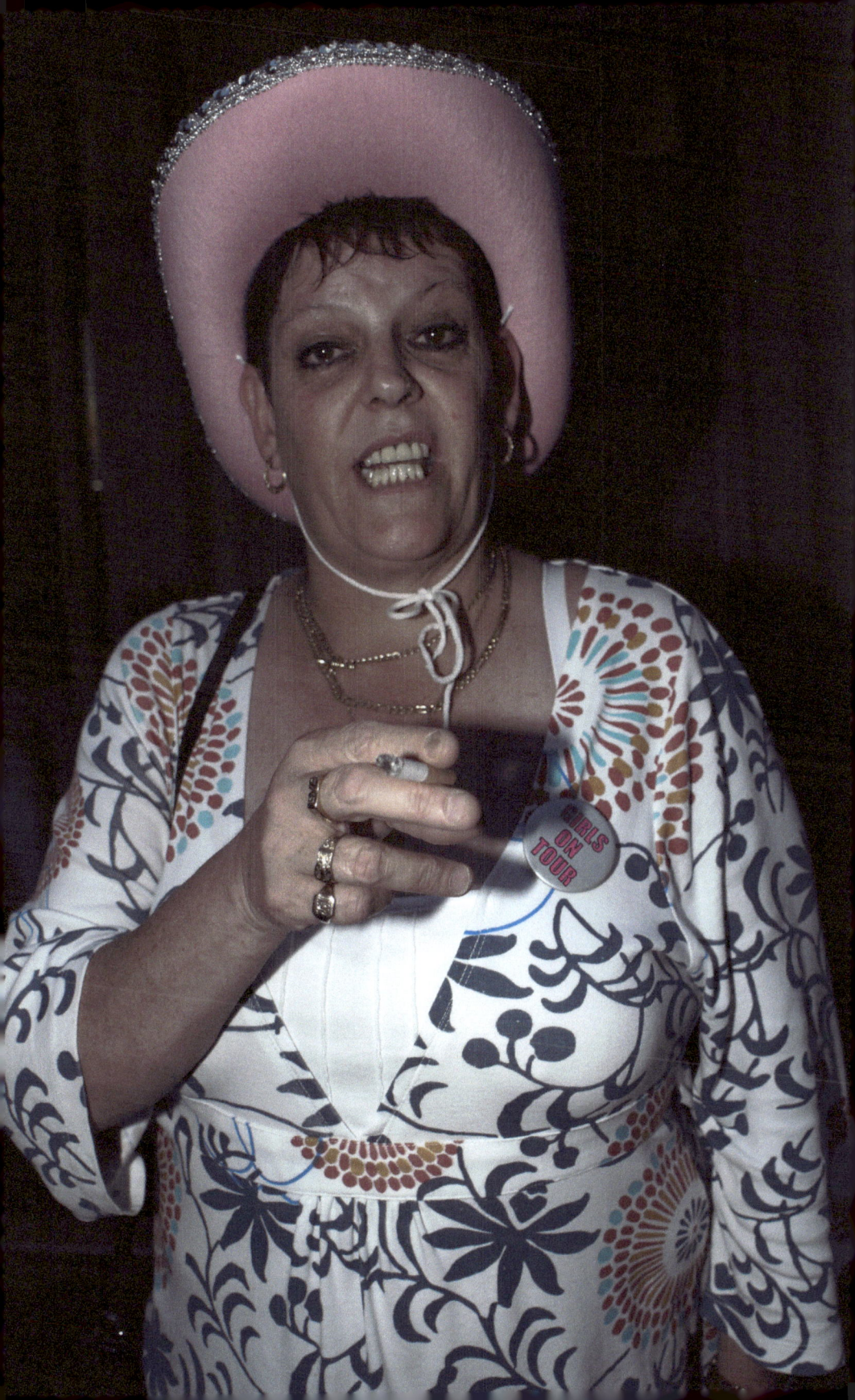

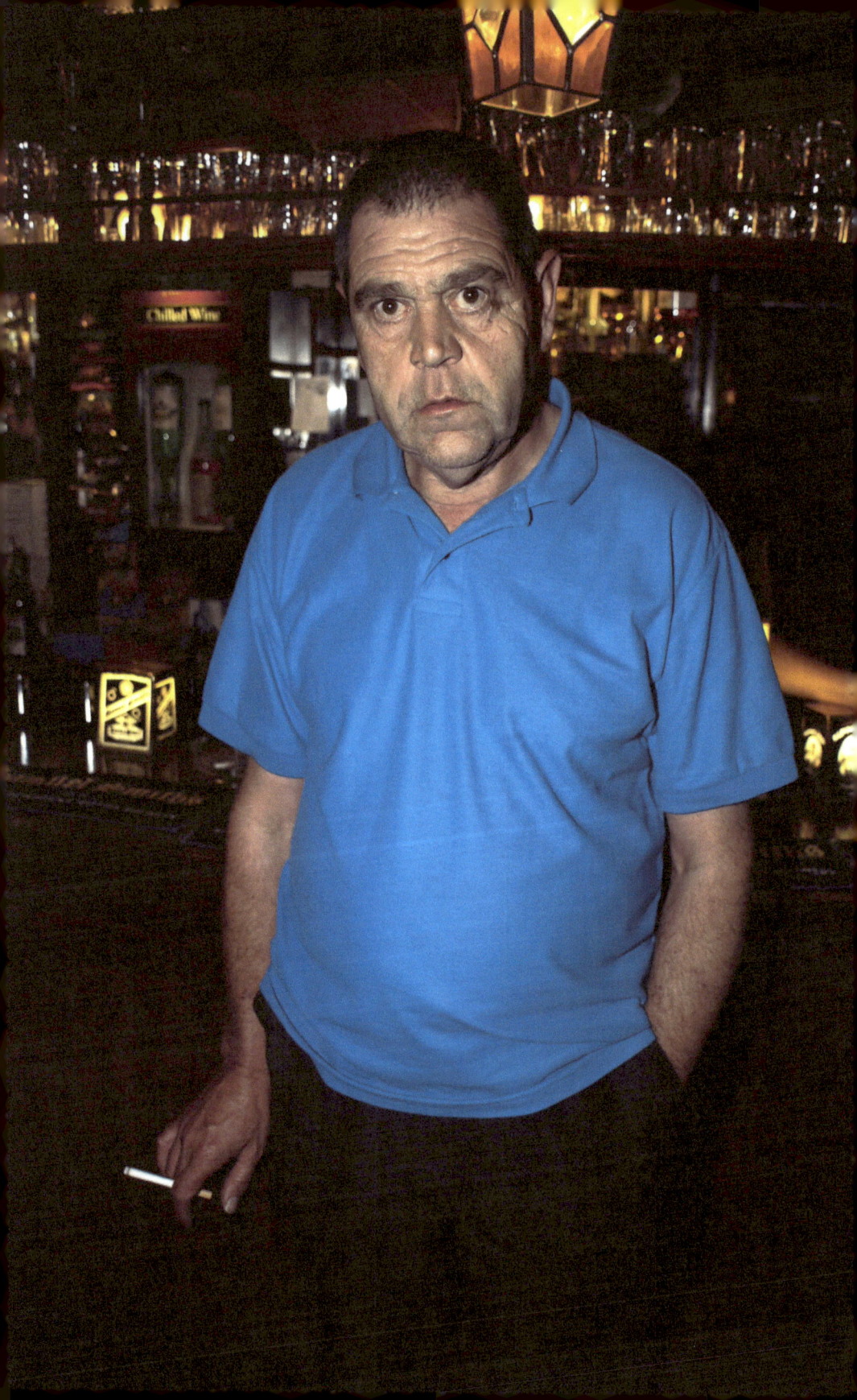

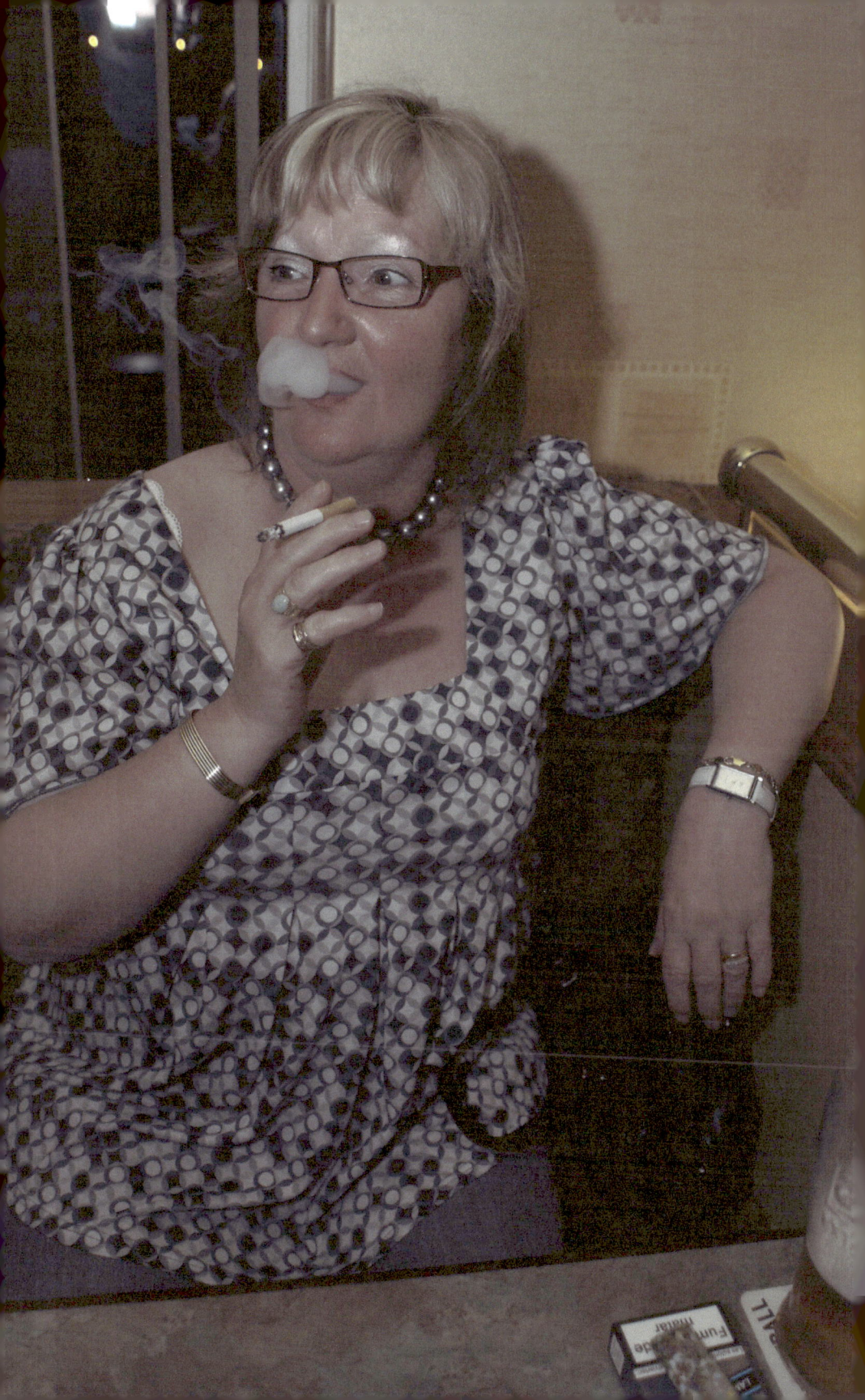

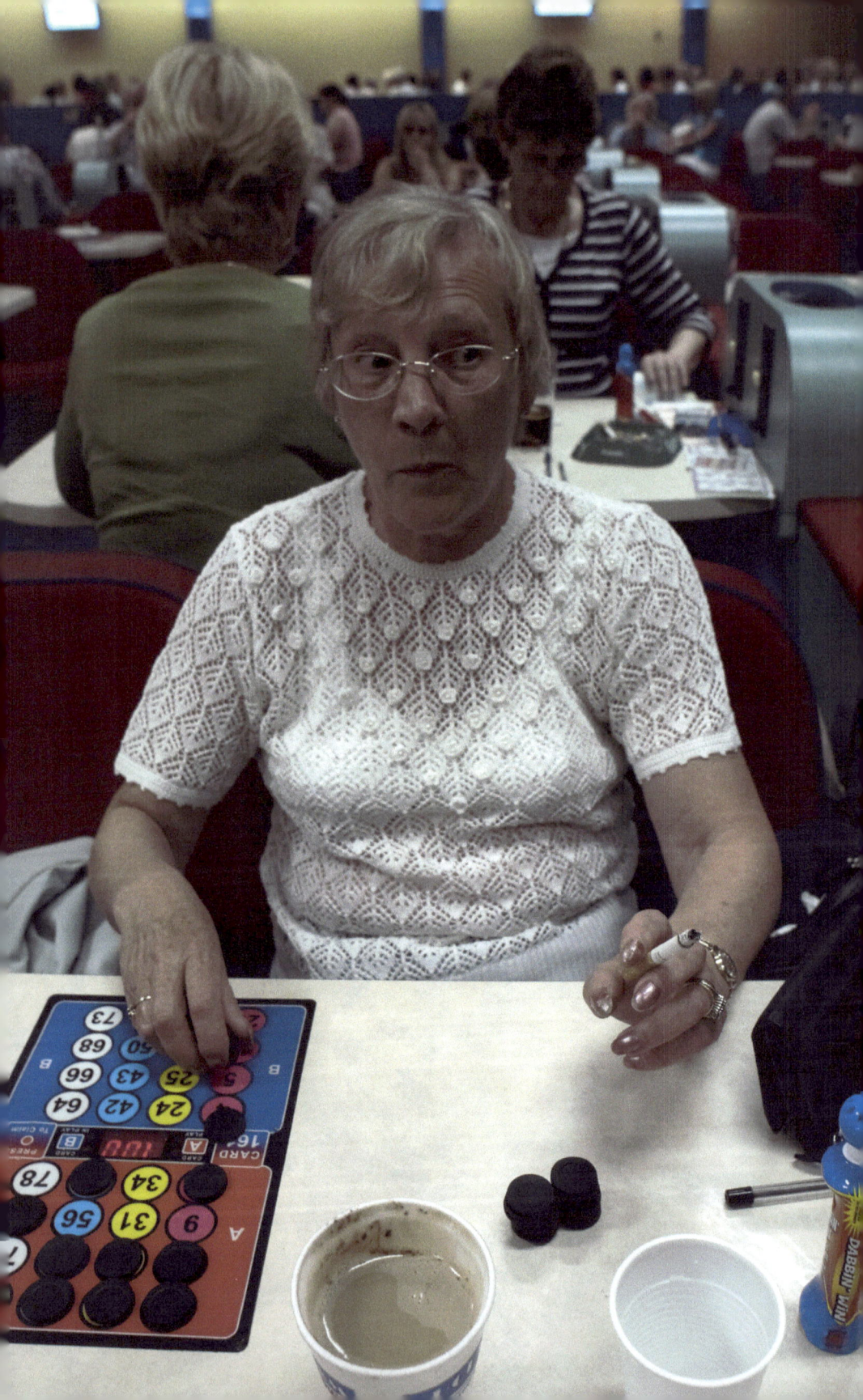

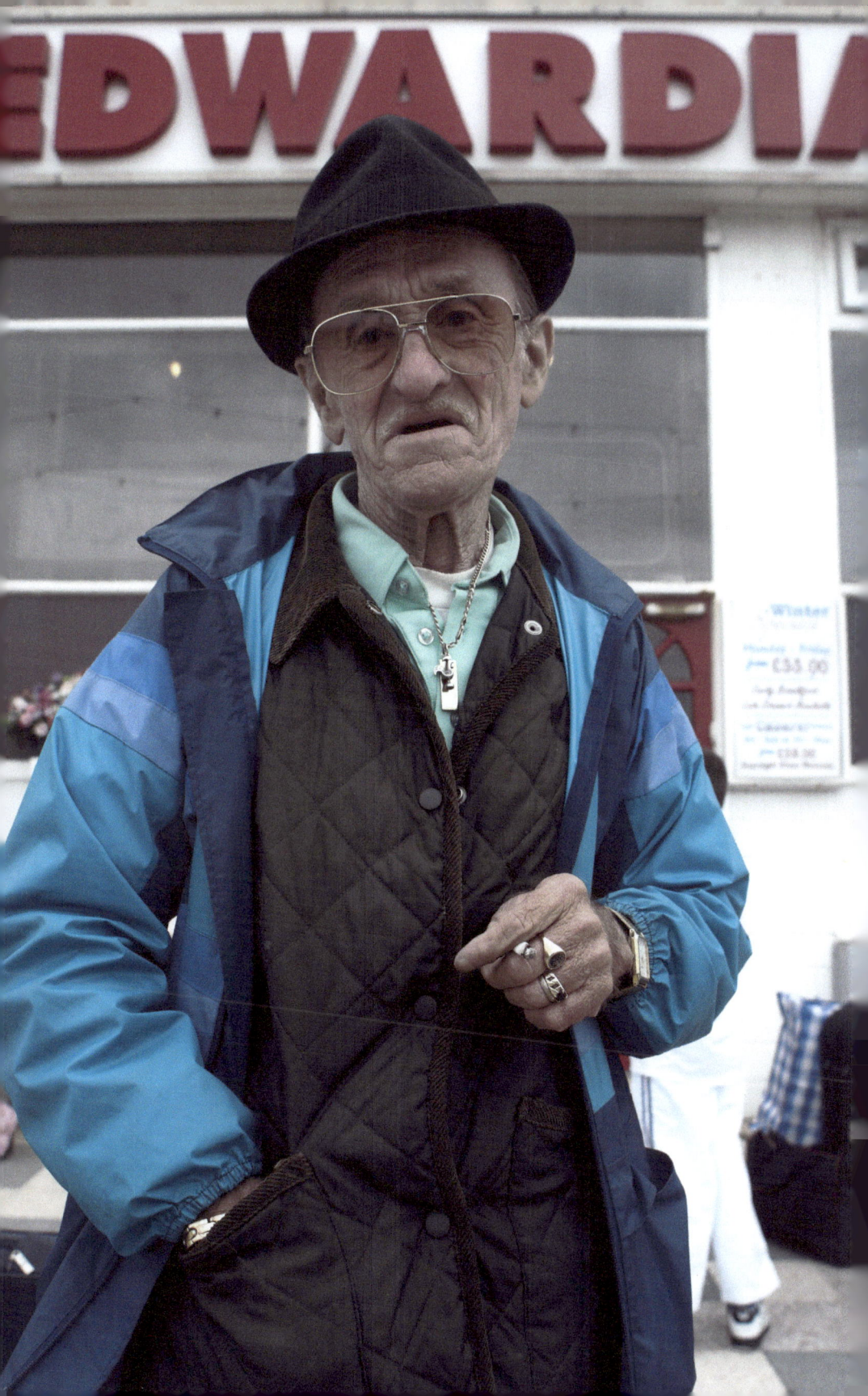

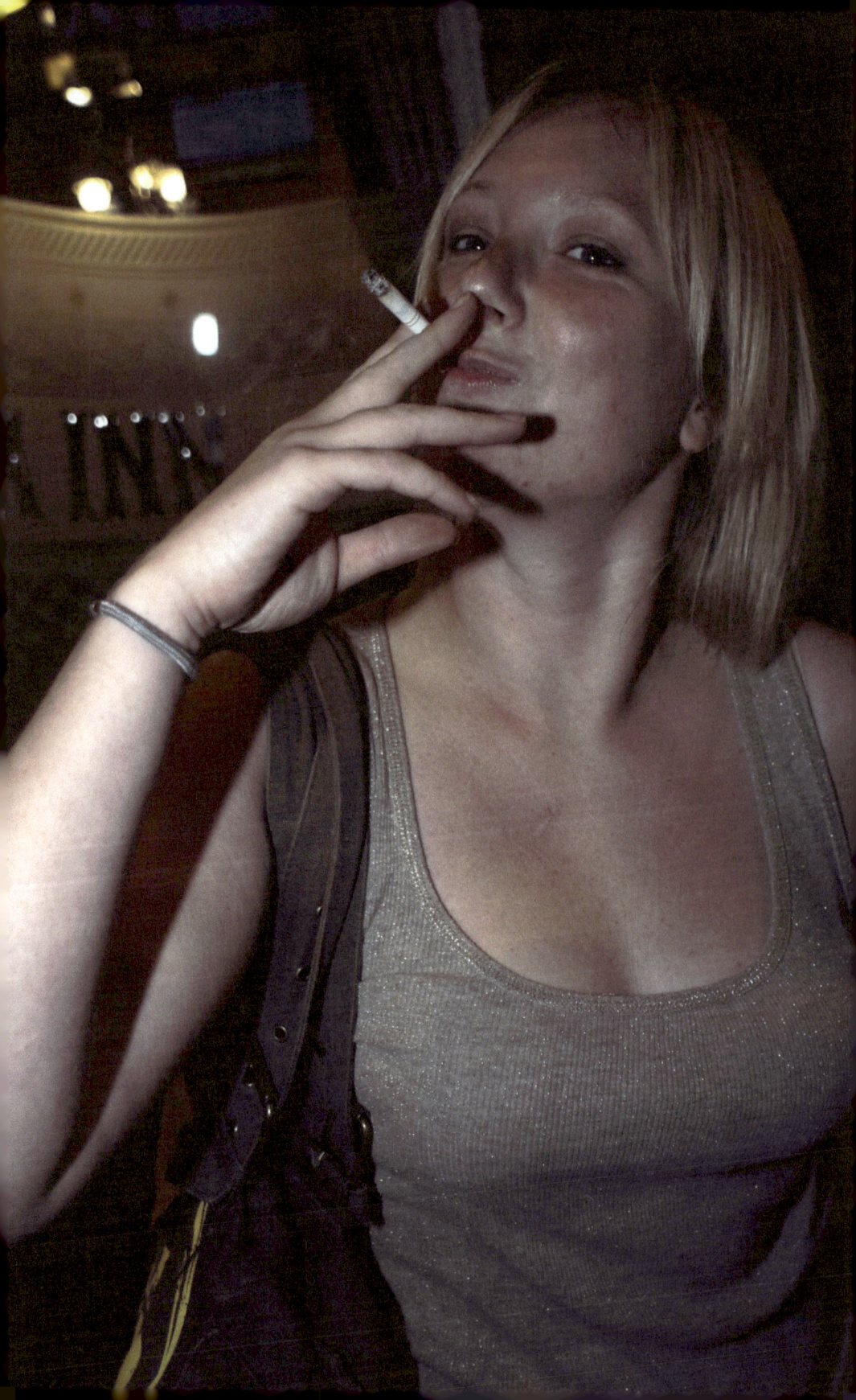

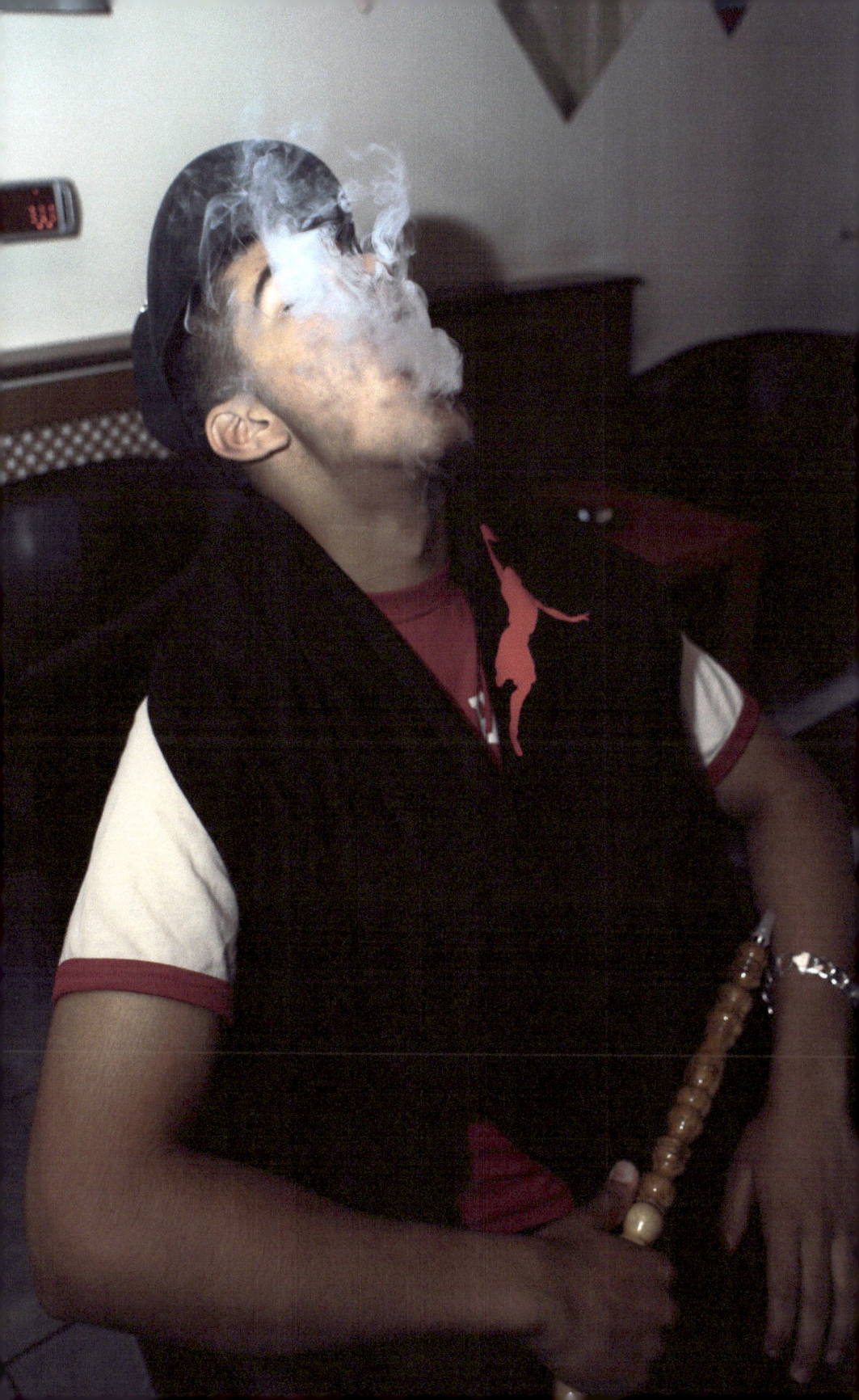

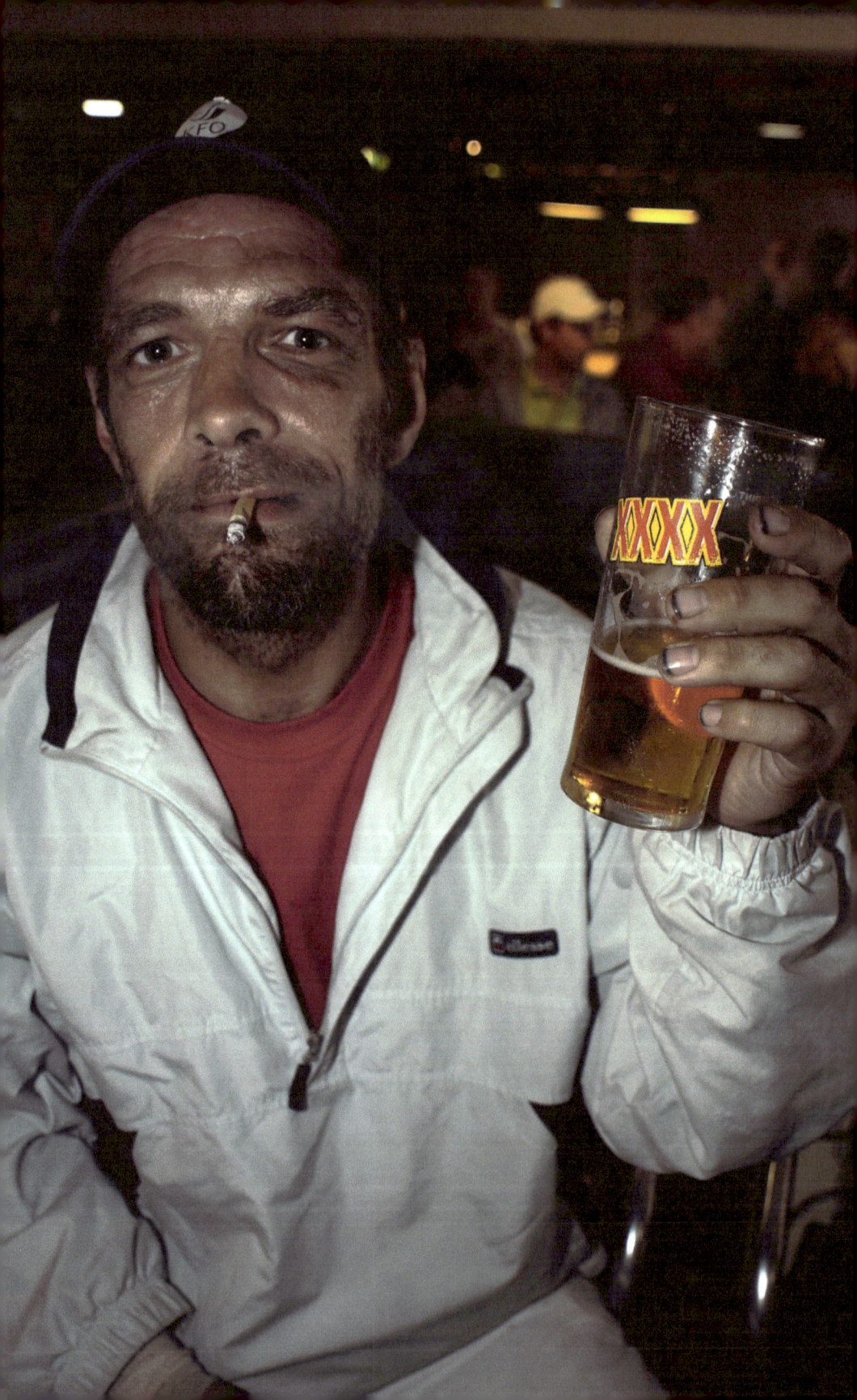

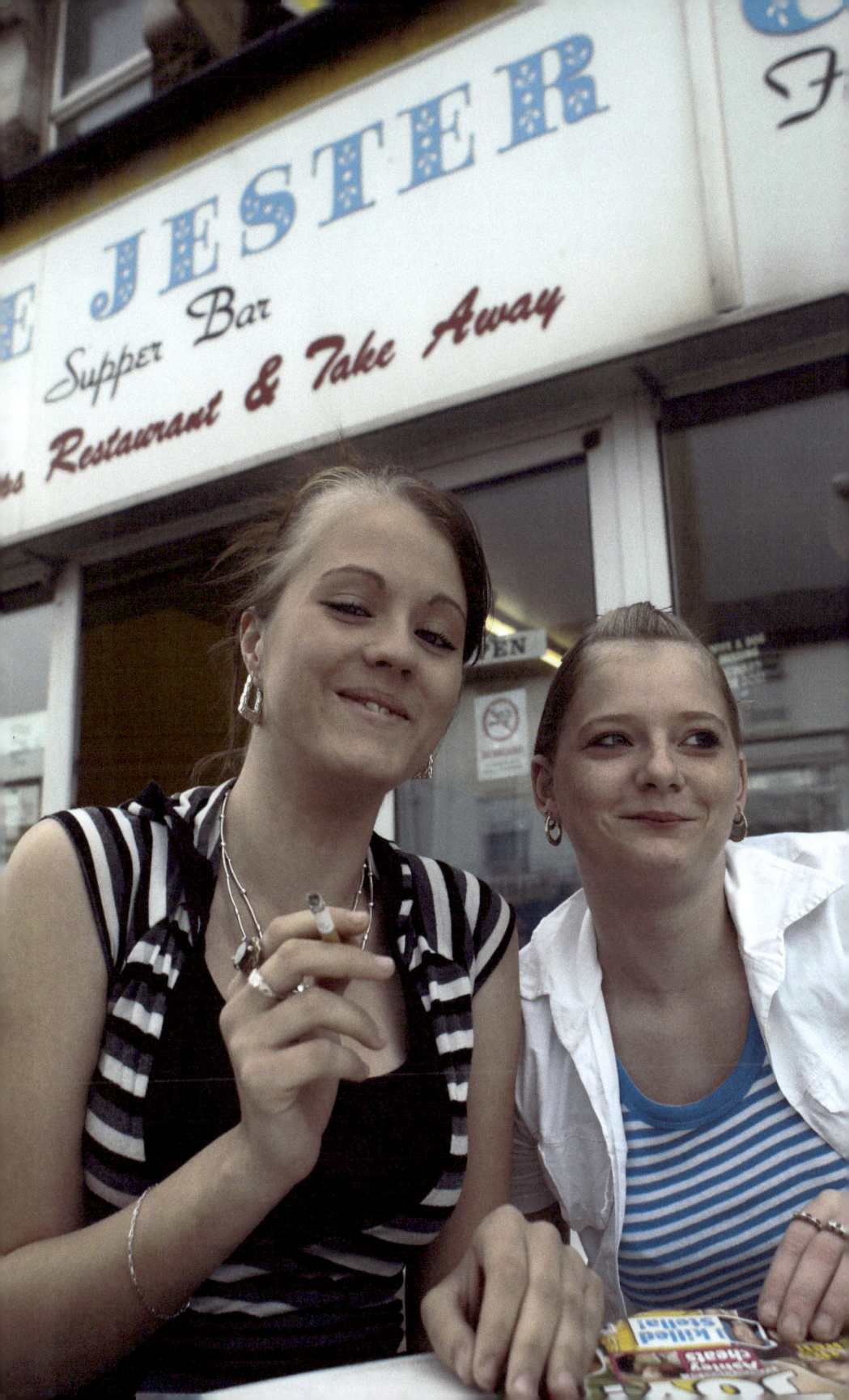

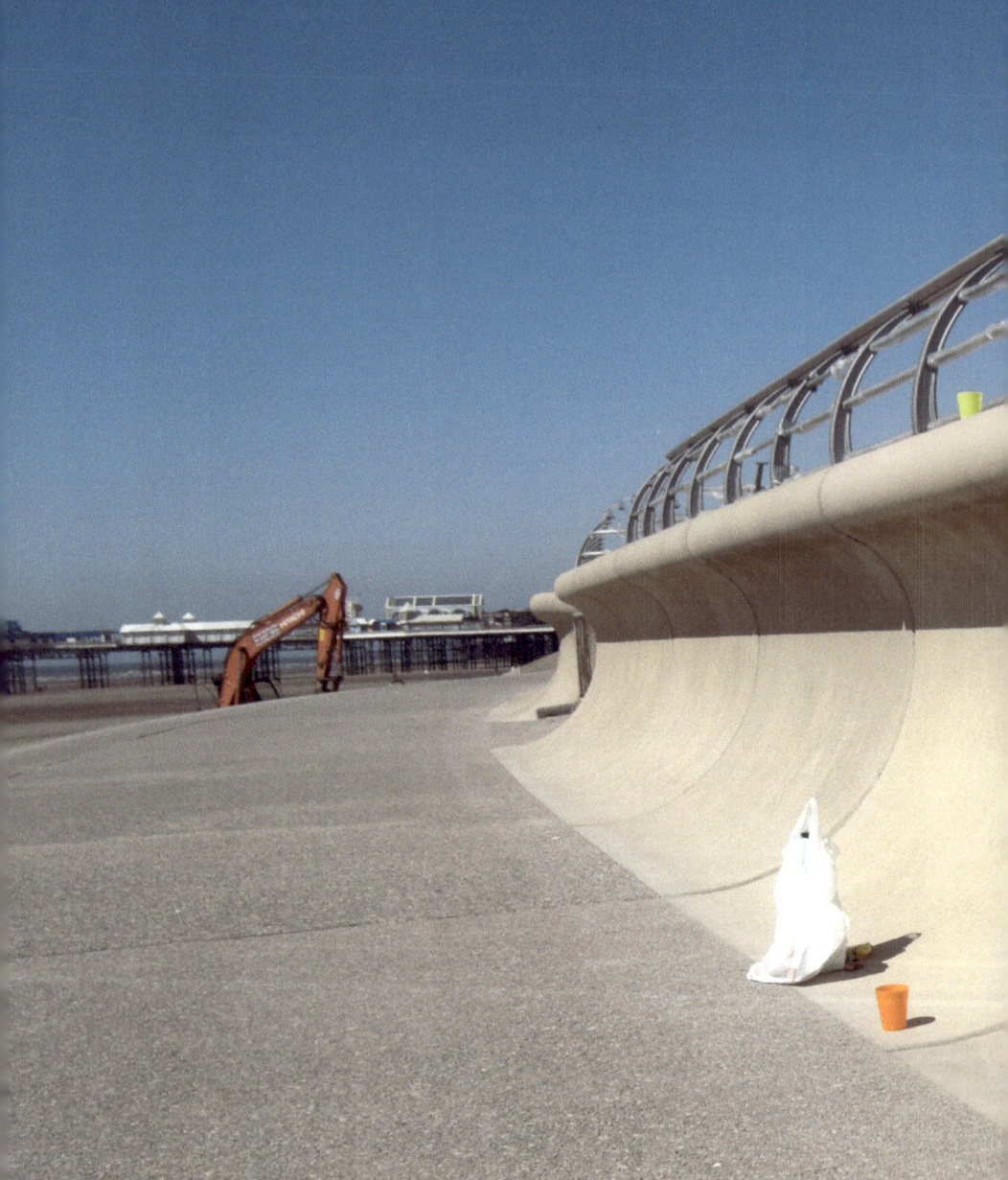

SUN, SEA AND SNAPS

VISIT BLACKPOOL

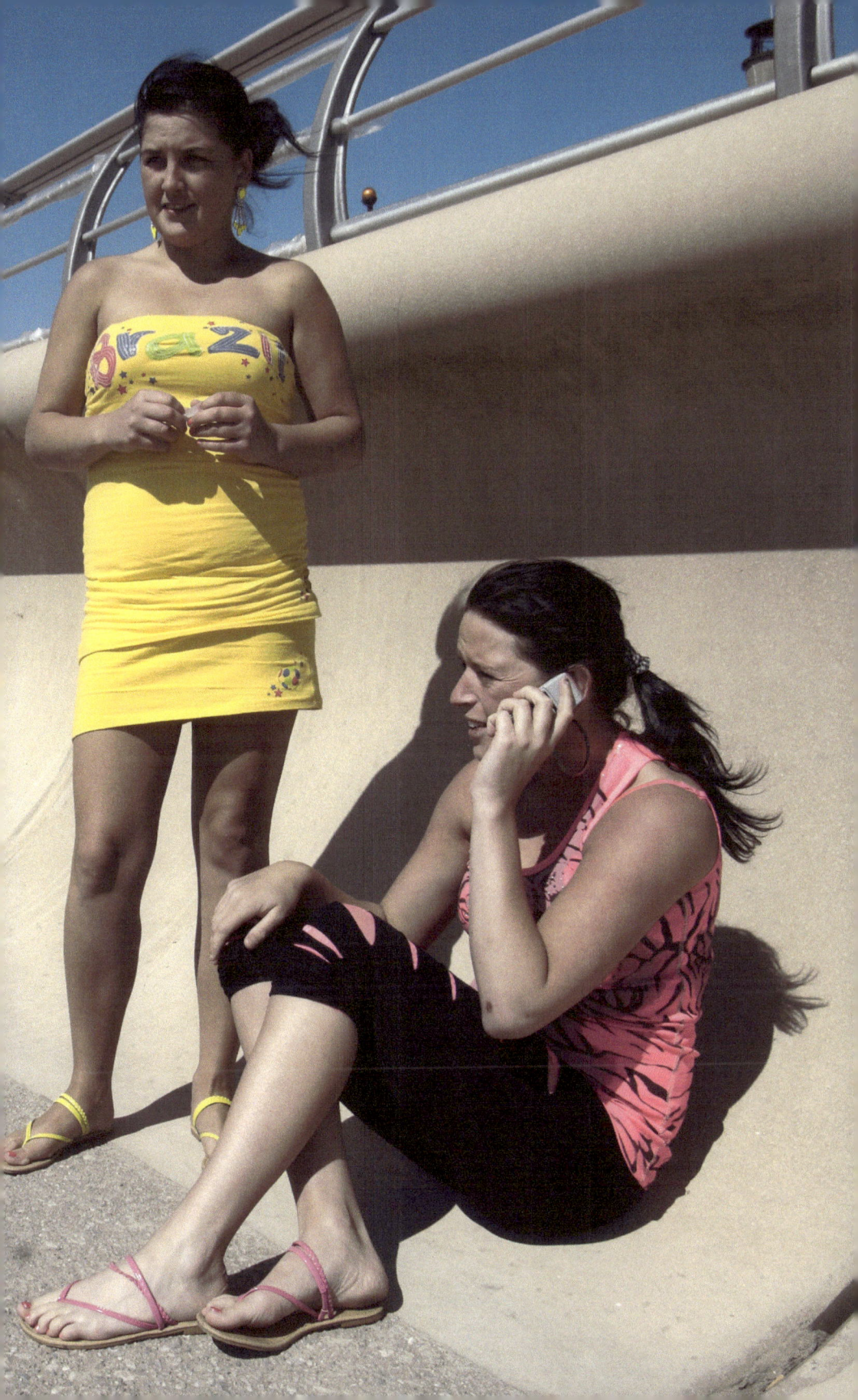

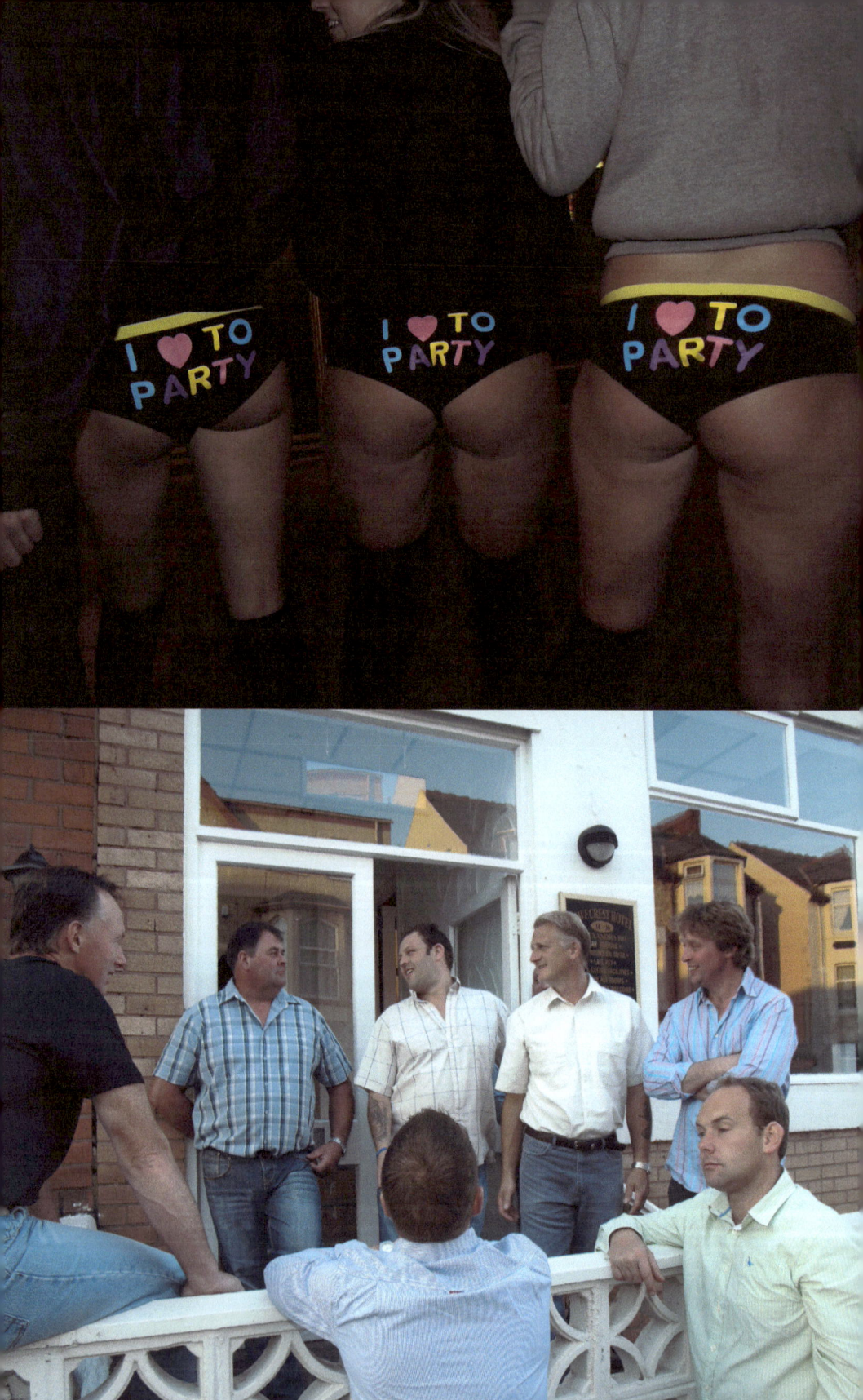

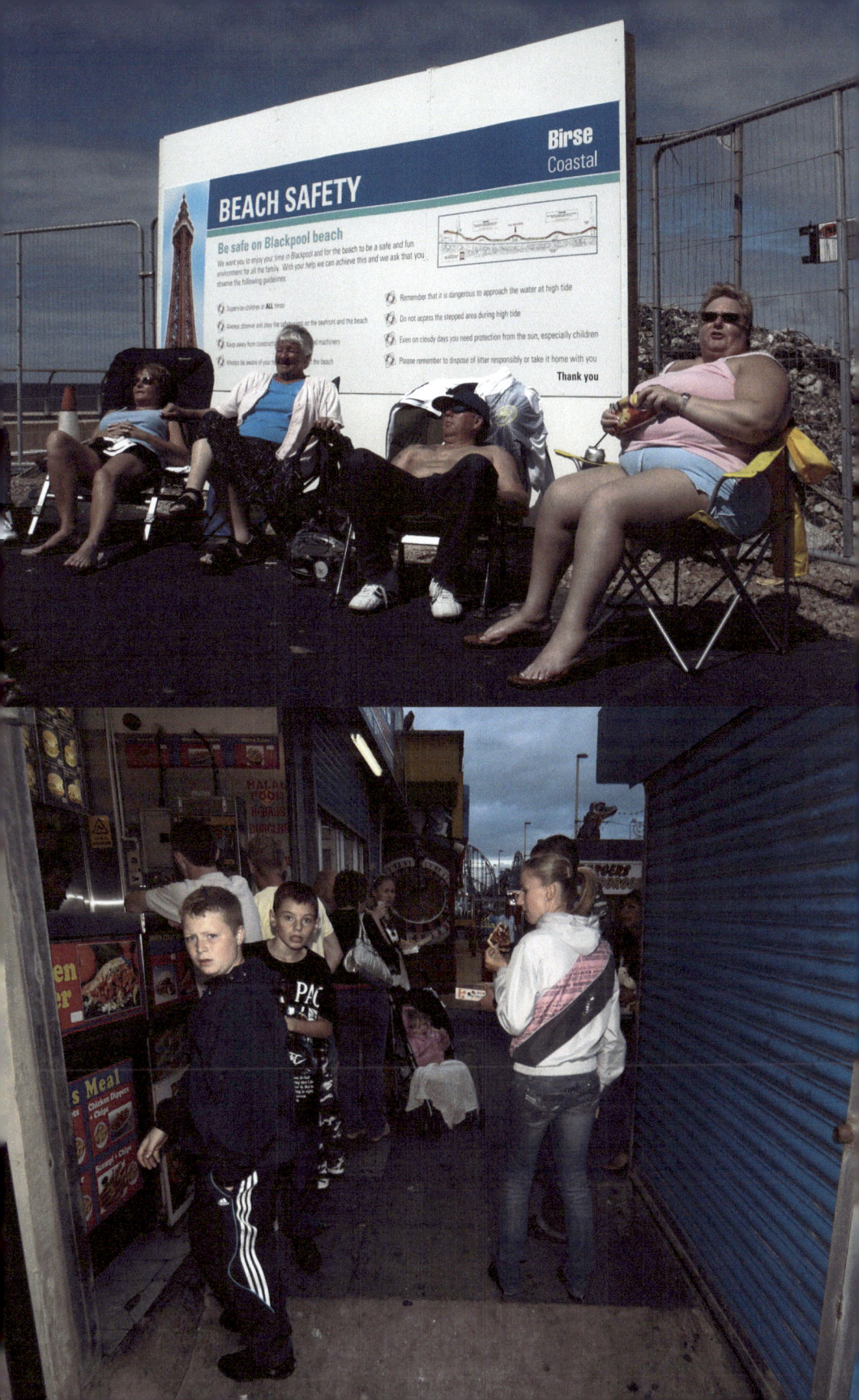

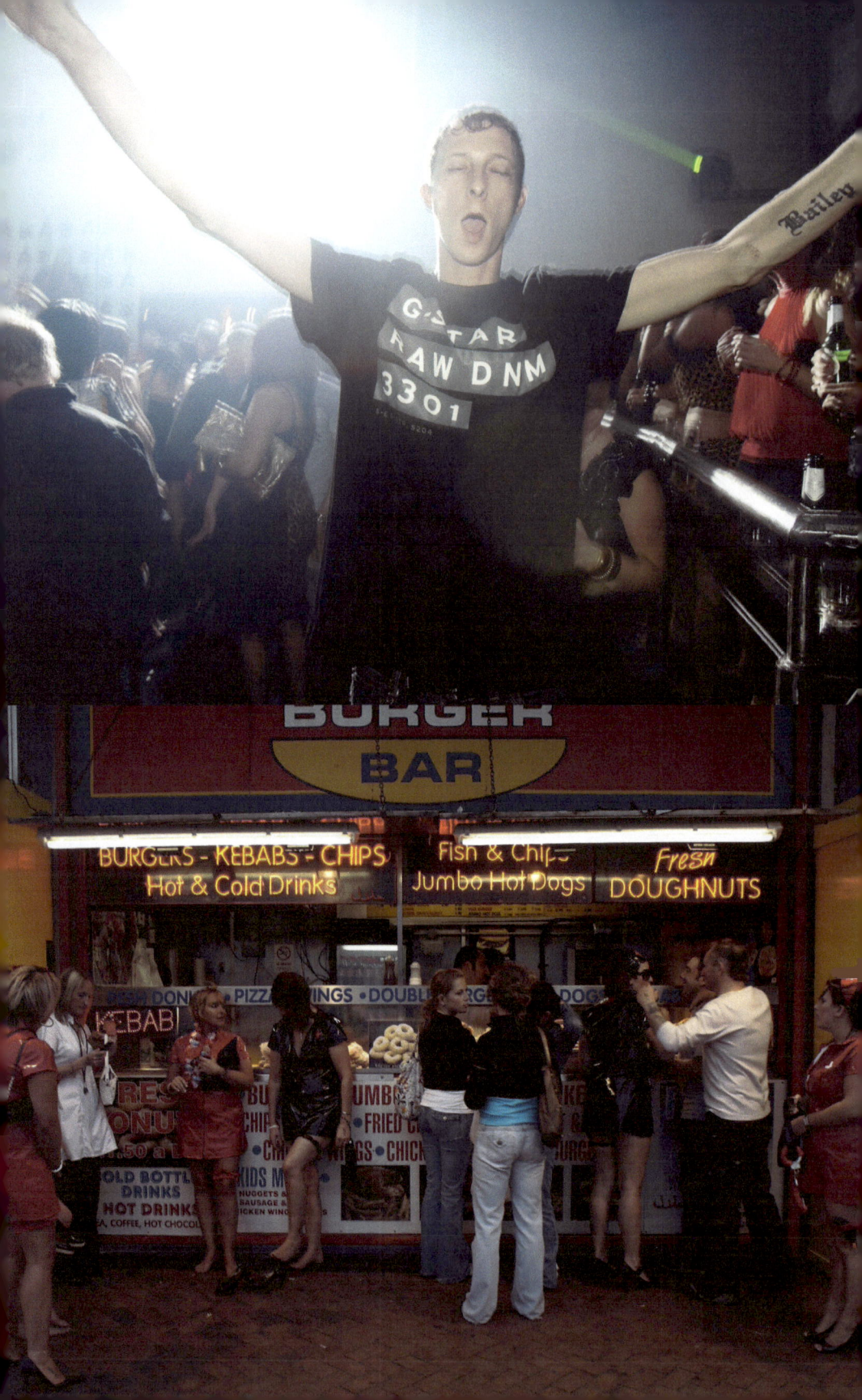

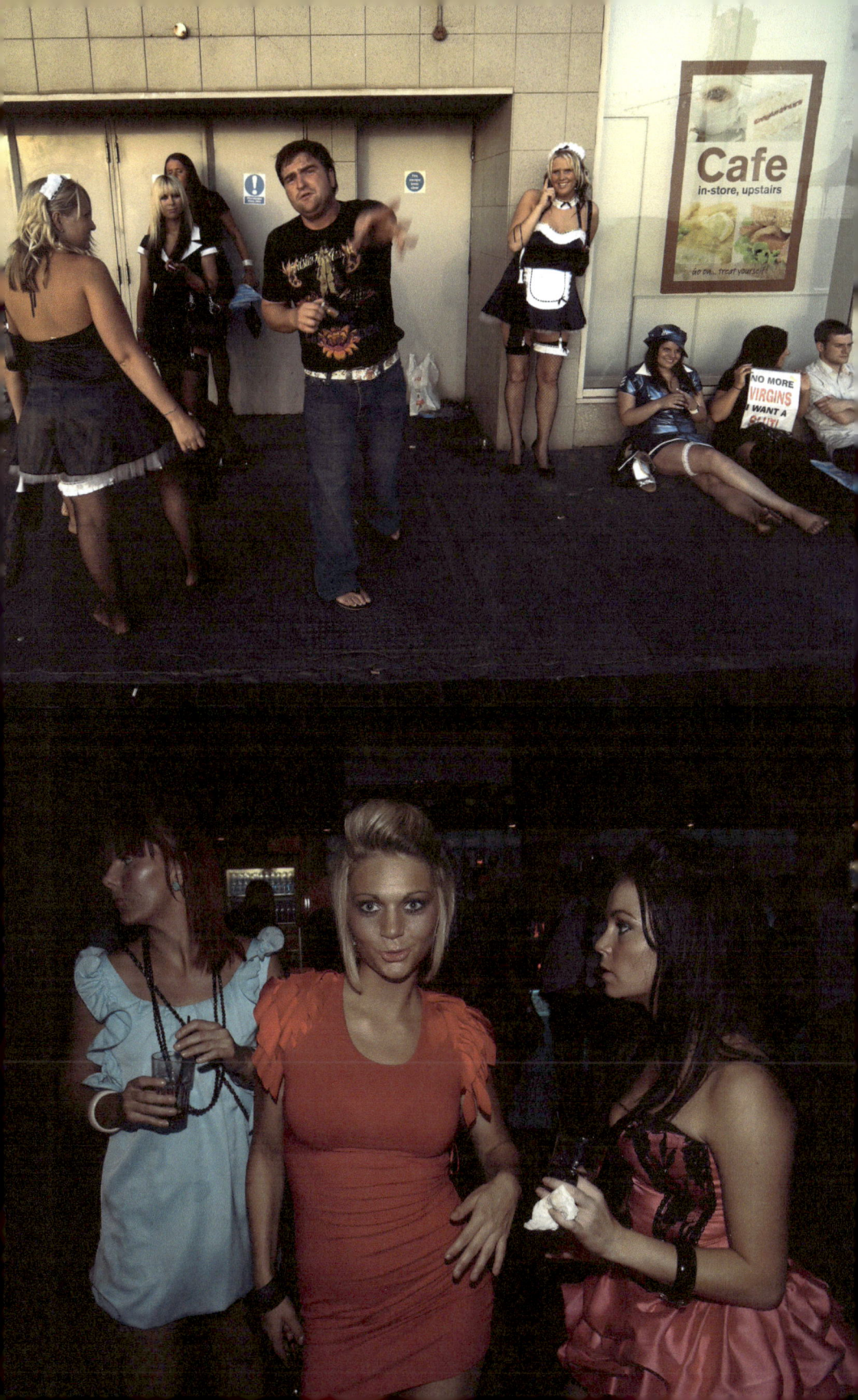

Dear Mum,

Having a great time in America! Spent the day with the Phelps' picketing outside a newspaper office, rival church and the local college. Loads of people hooted their horns in disgust but all the Westboro Baptist Church kids love it.
Love Garry

BLOT ART · Golden Hill Craft Centre · Freshwater · Isle of Wight · PO40 9TF

Me Mam
Newcastle
North - east England
United Kingdom

God Hates America

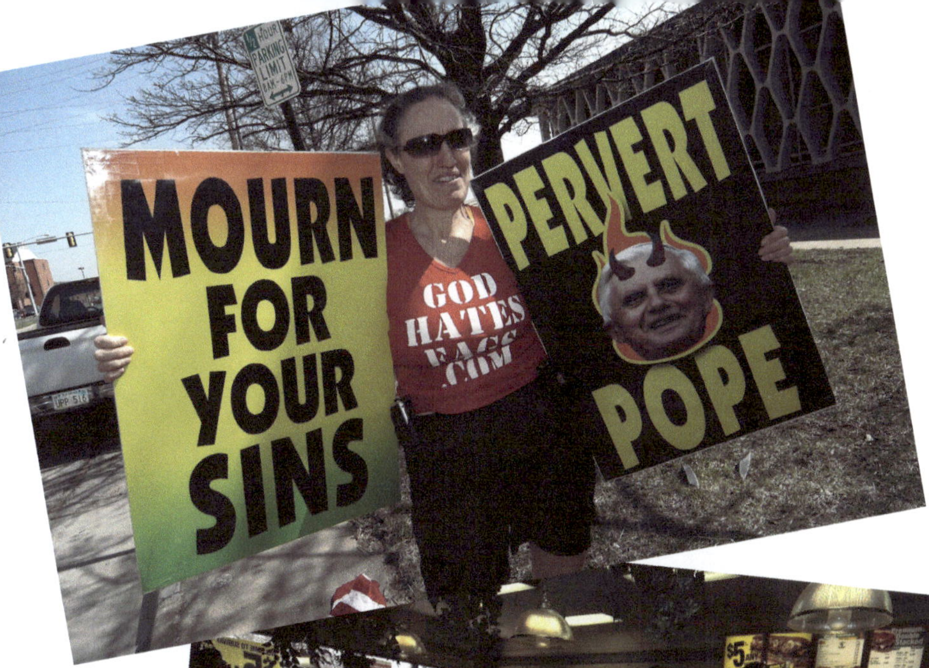

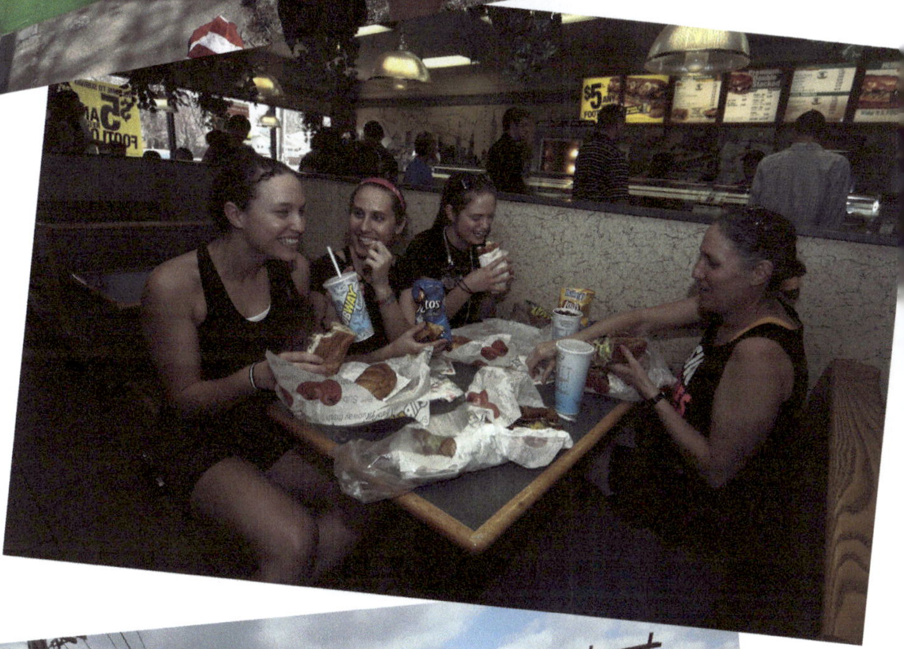

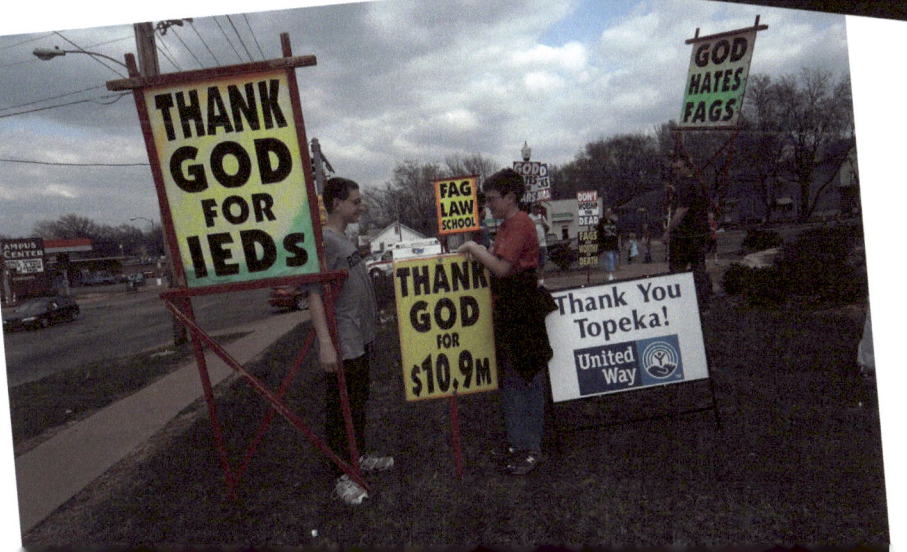

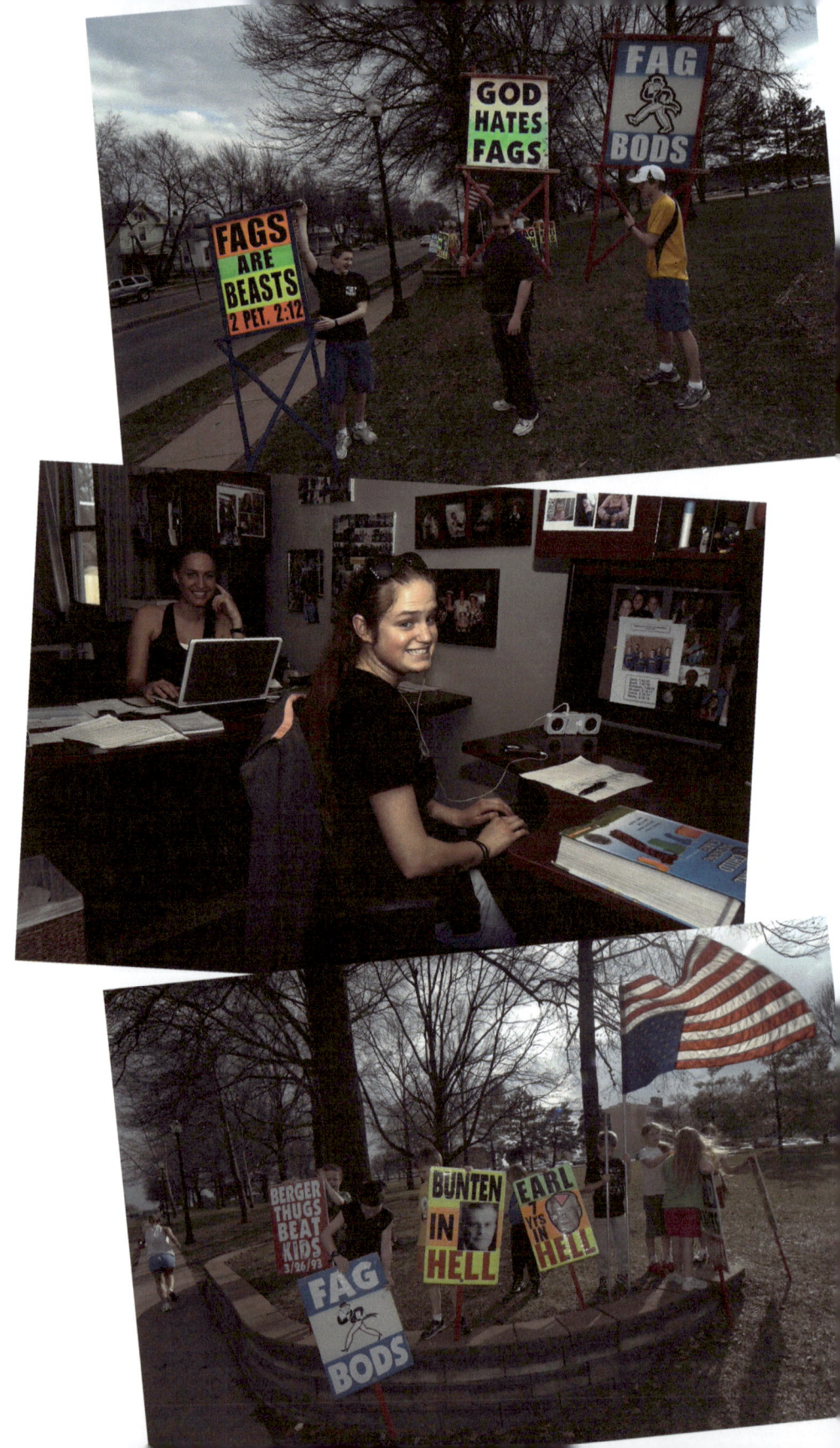

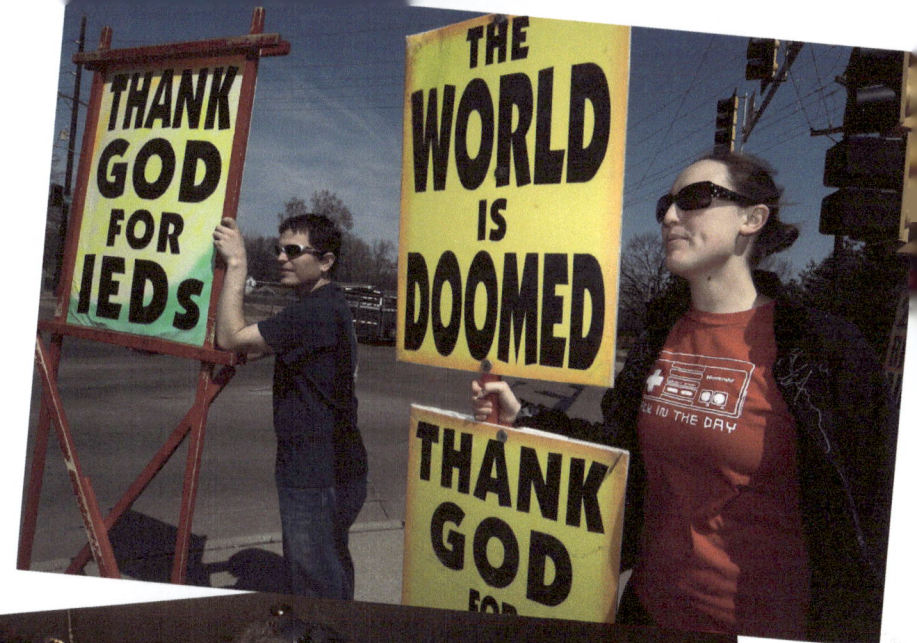

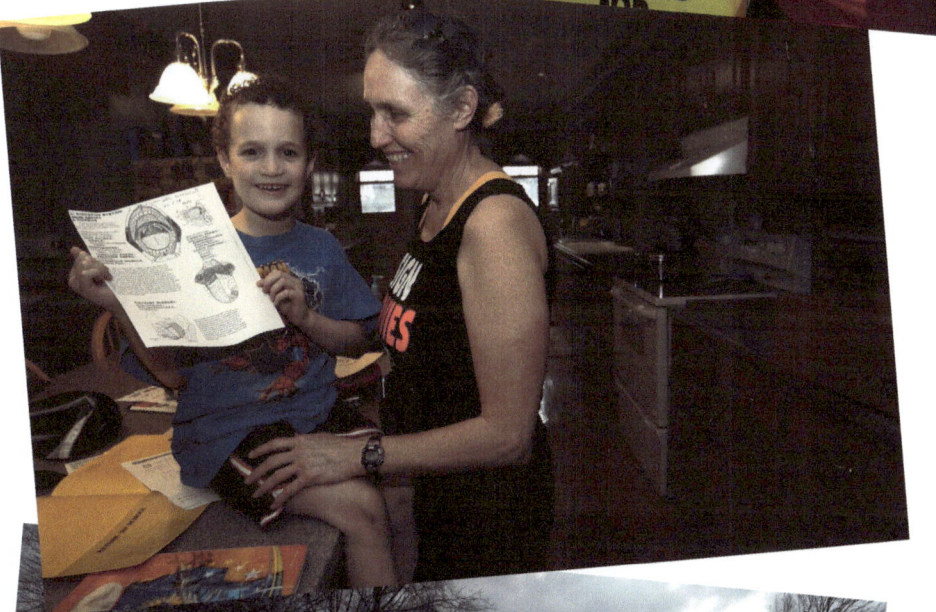

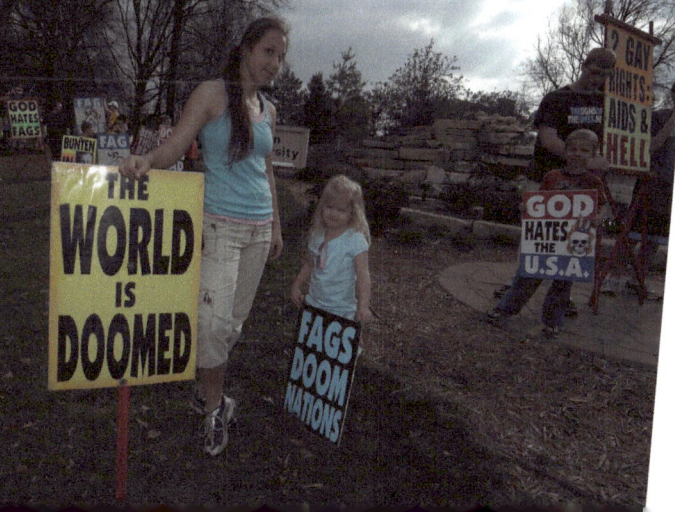

Bethlehem

History, faith, religion
Come and see the walled city

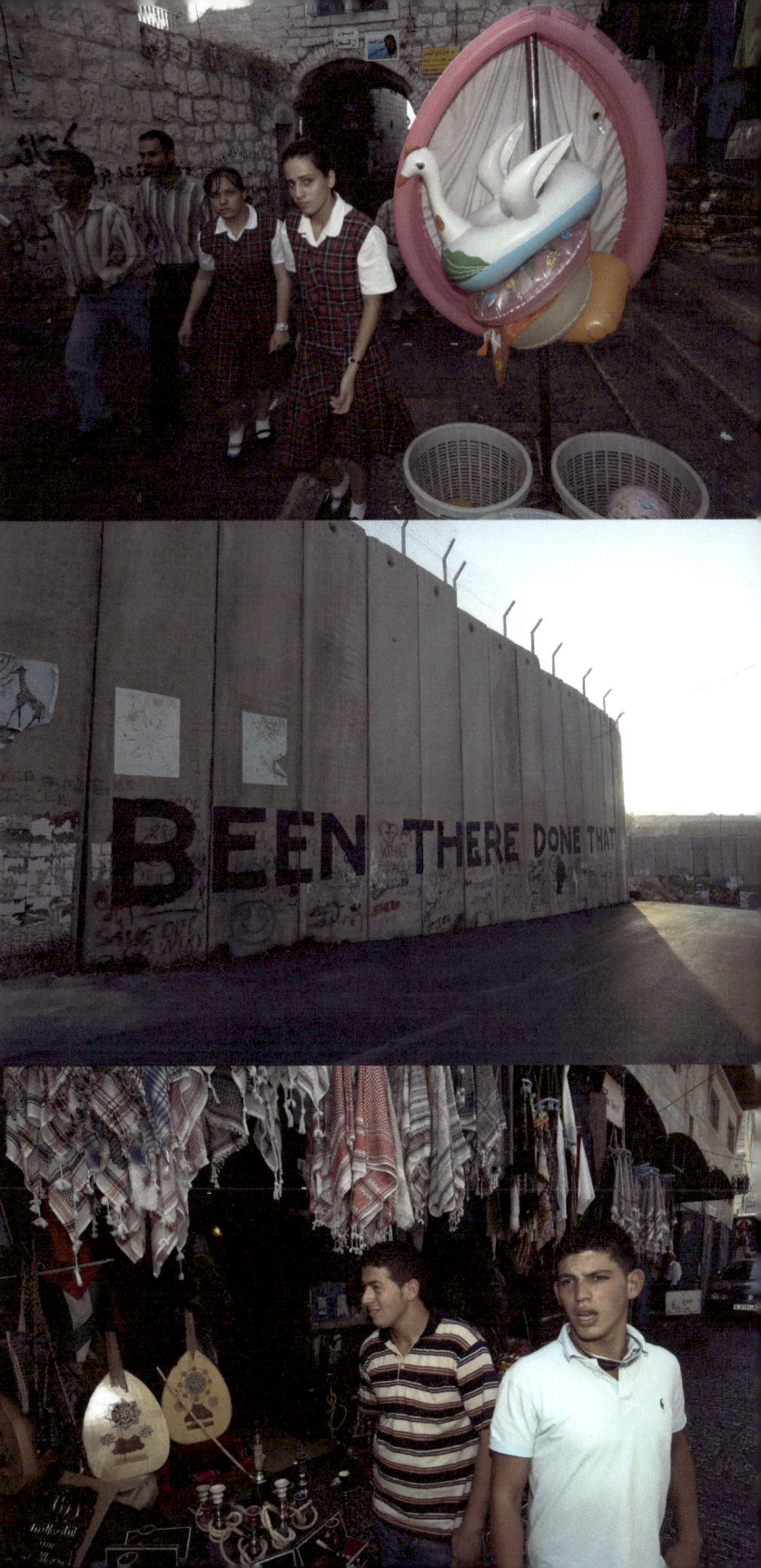

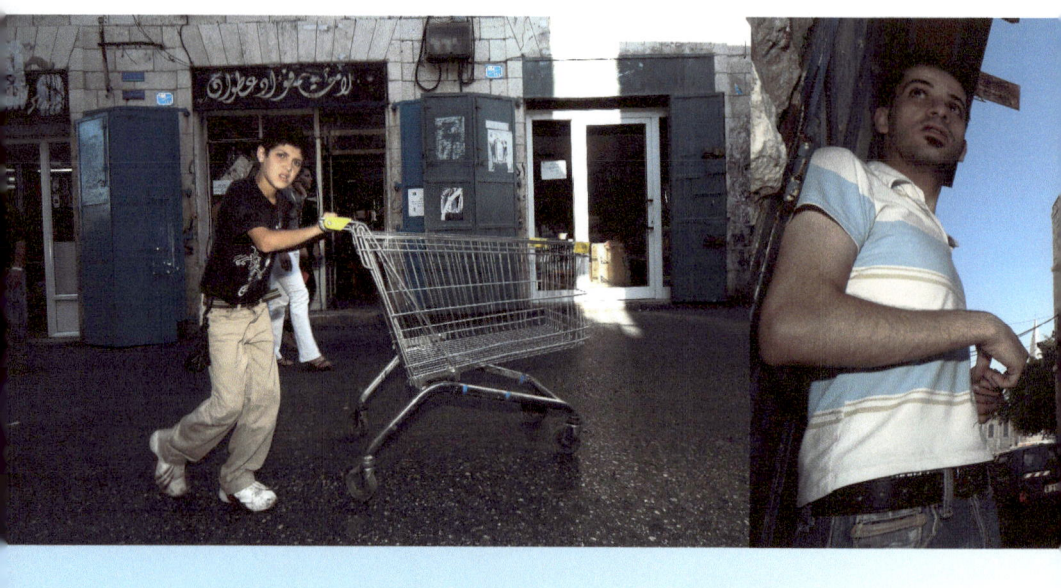

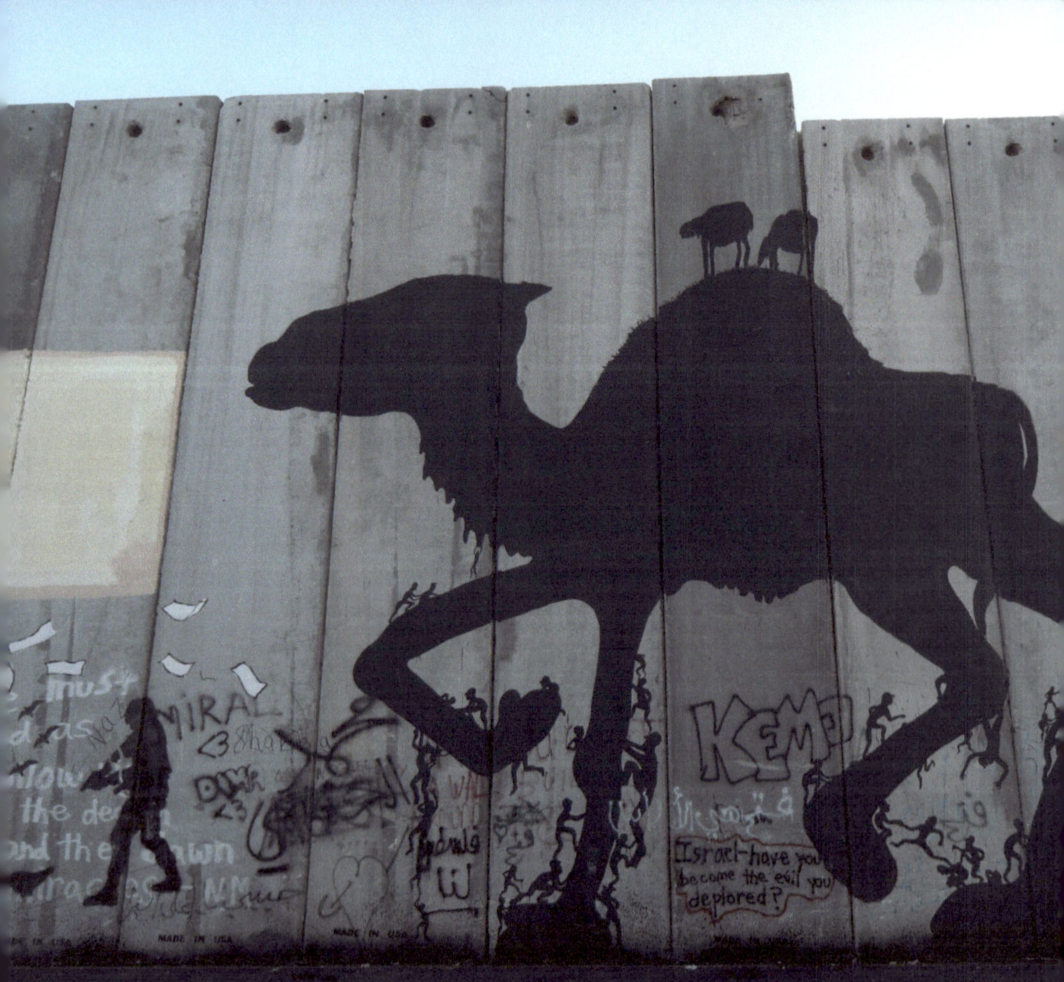

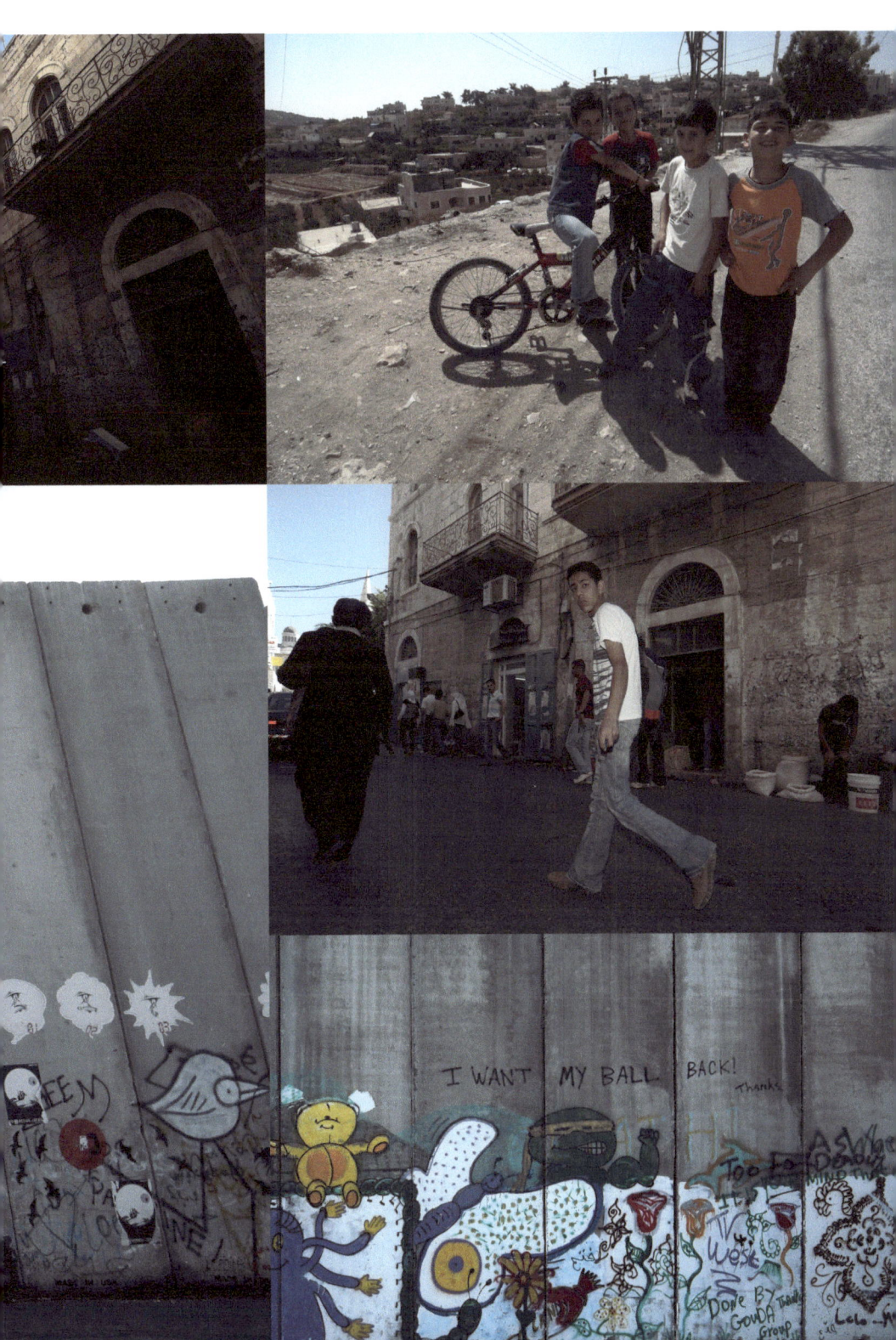

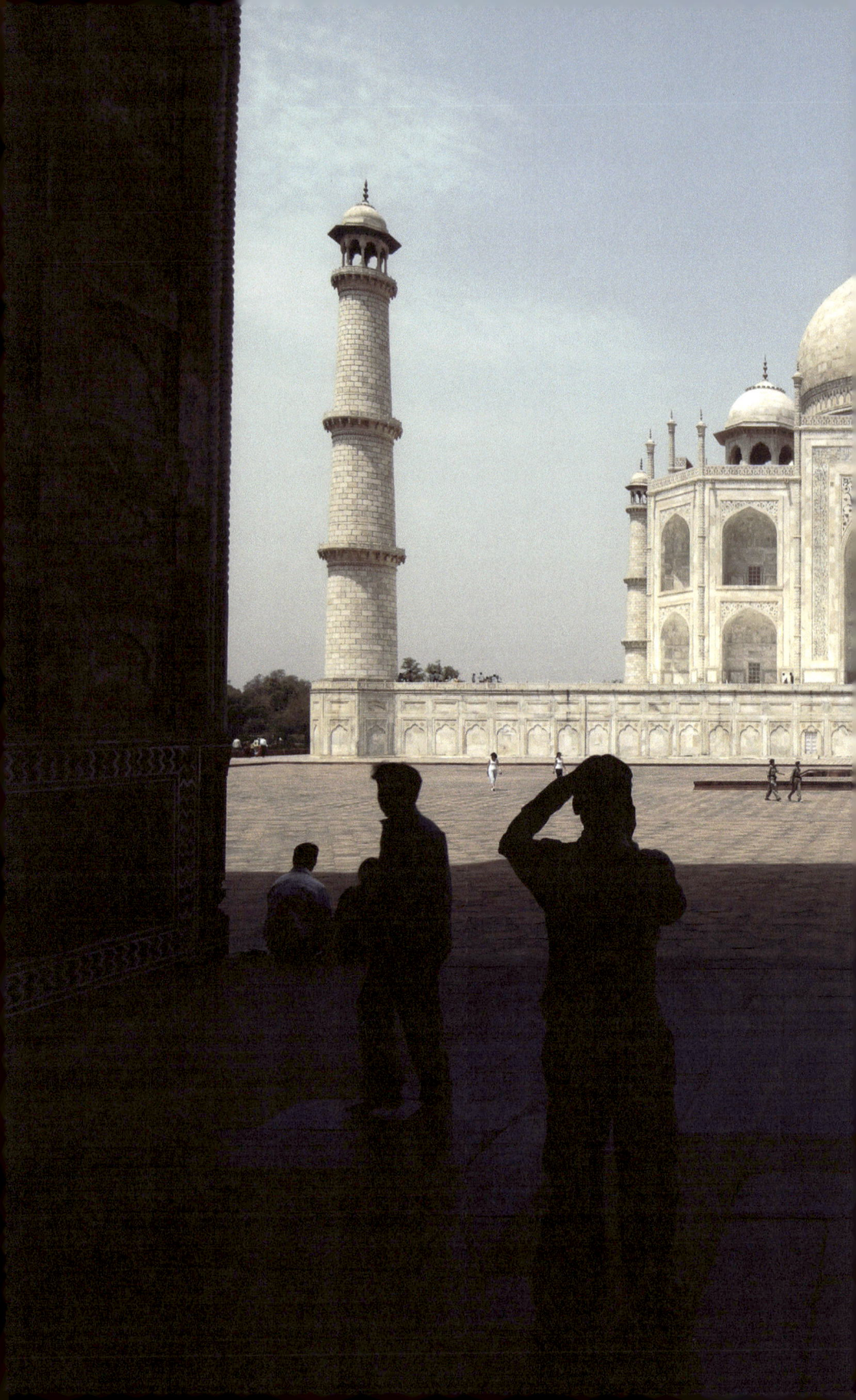

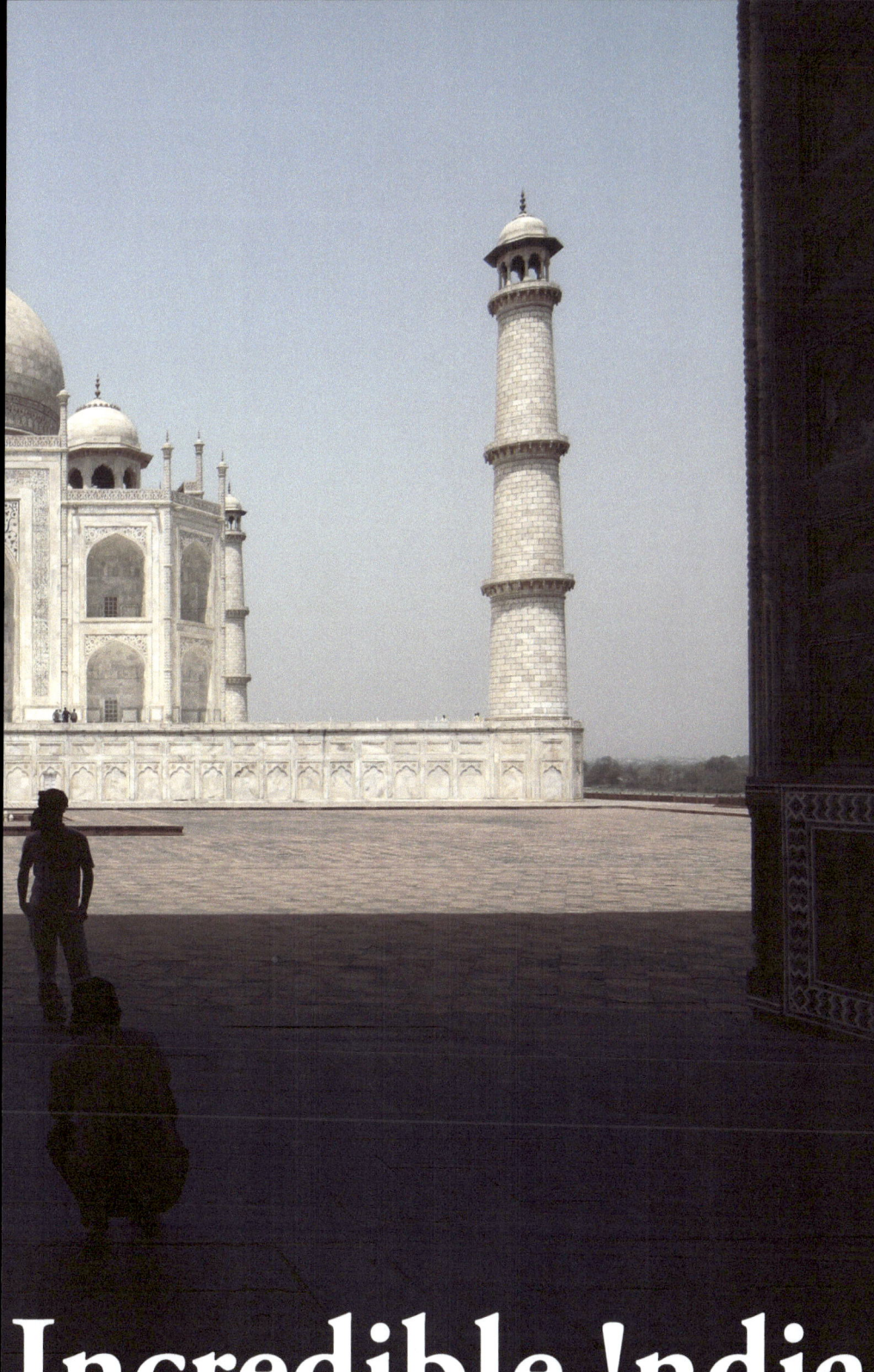

Incredible !ndia

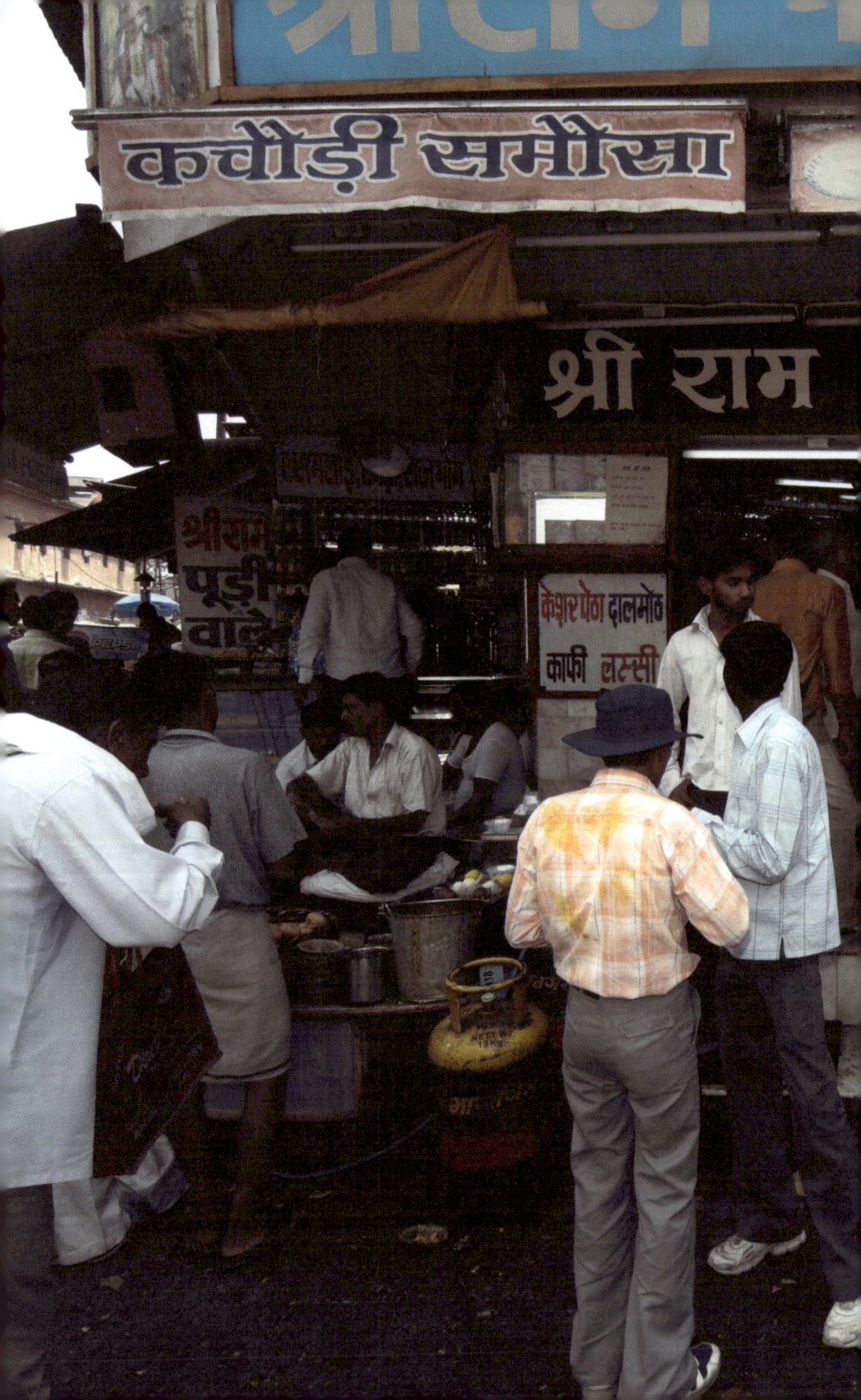

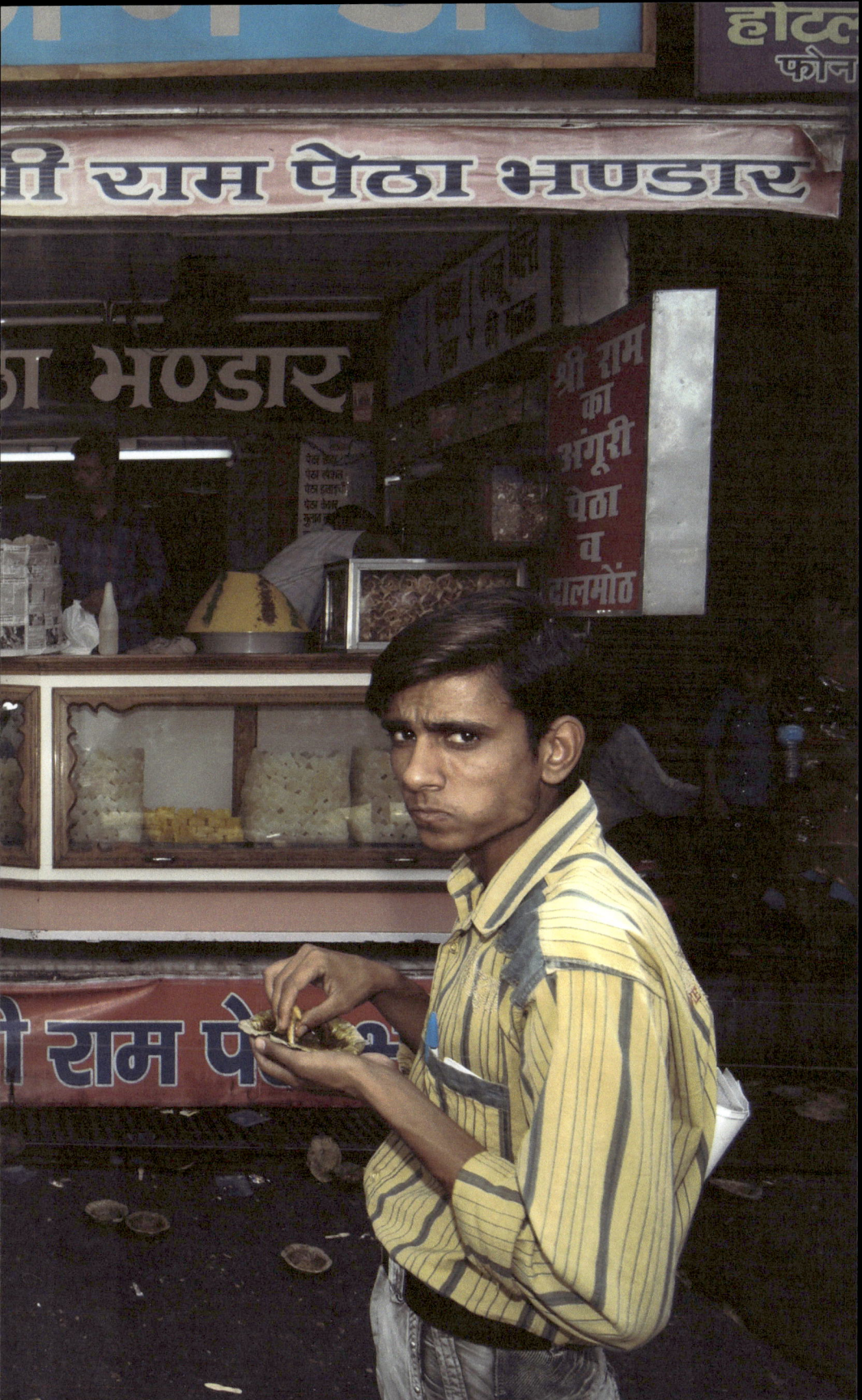

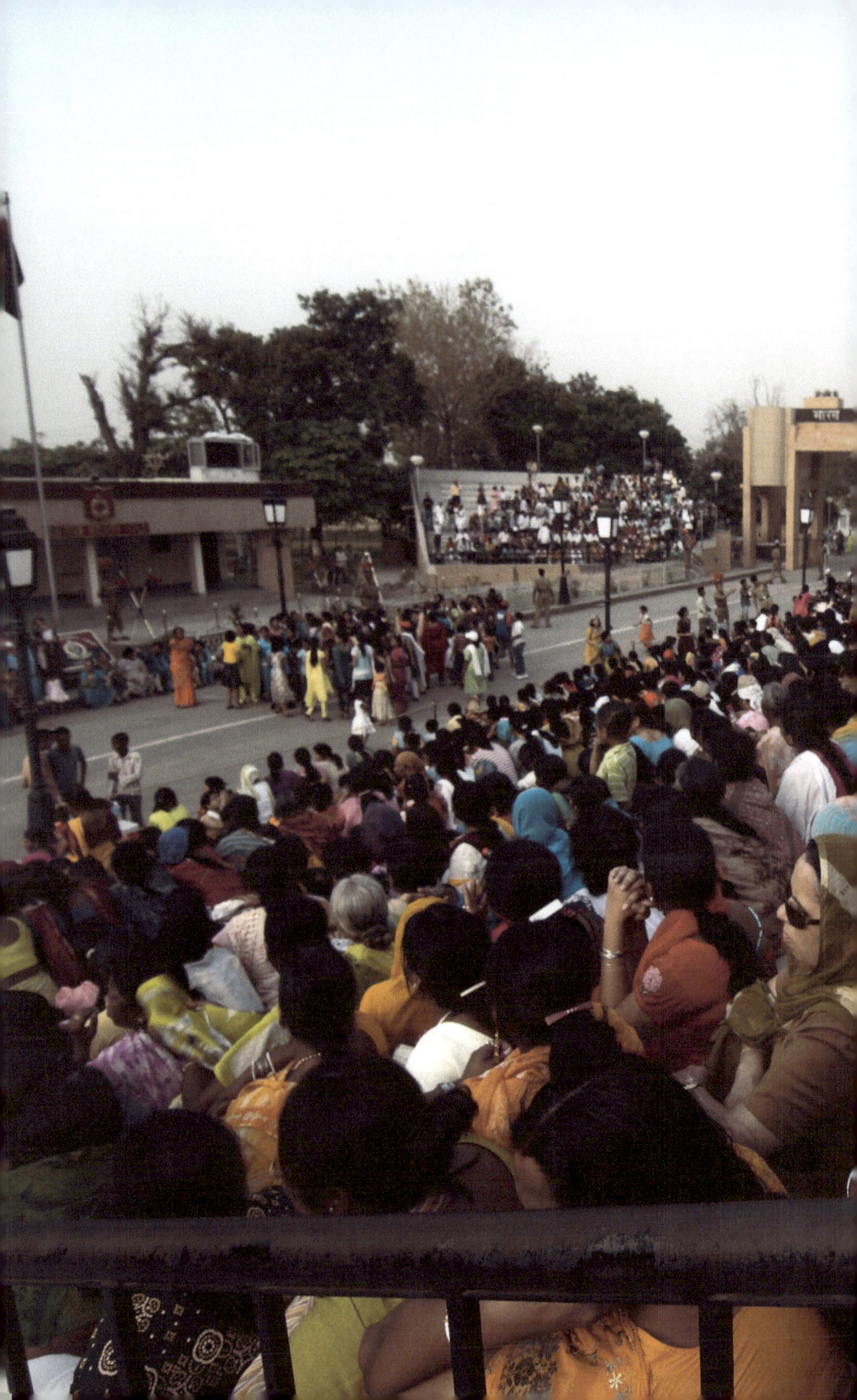

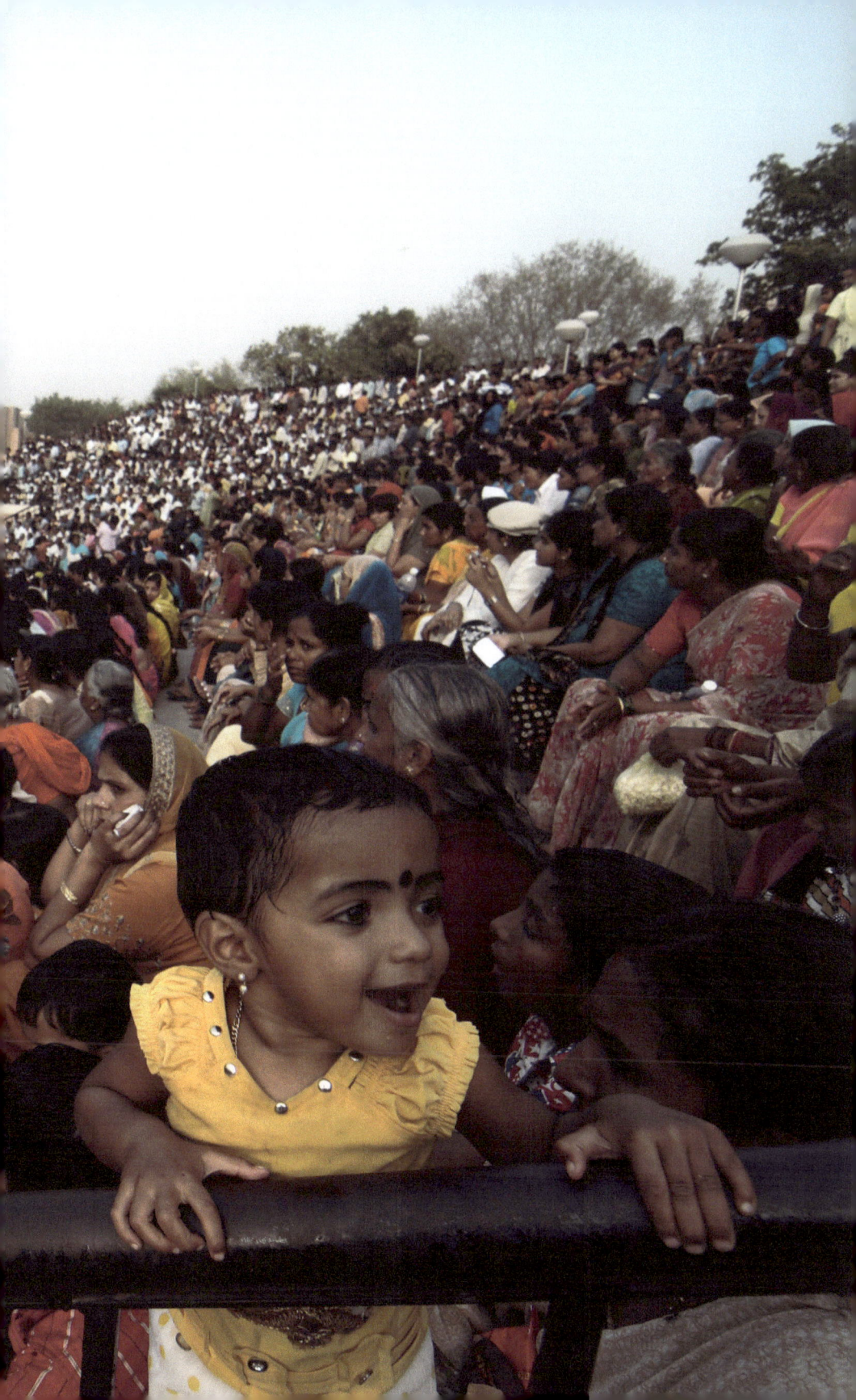

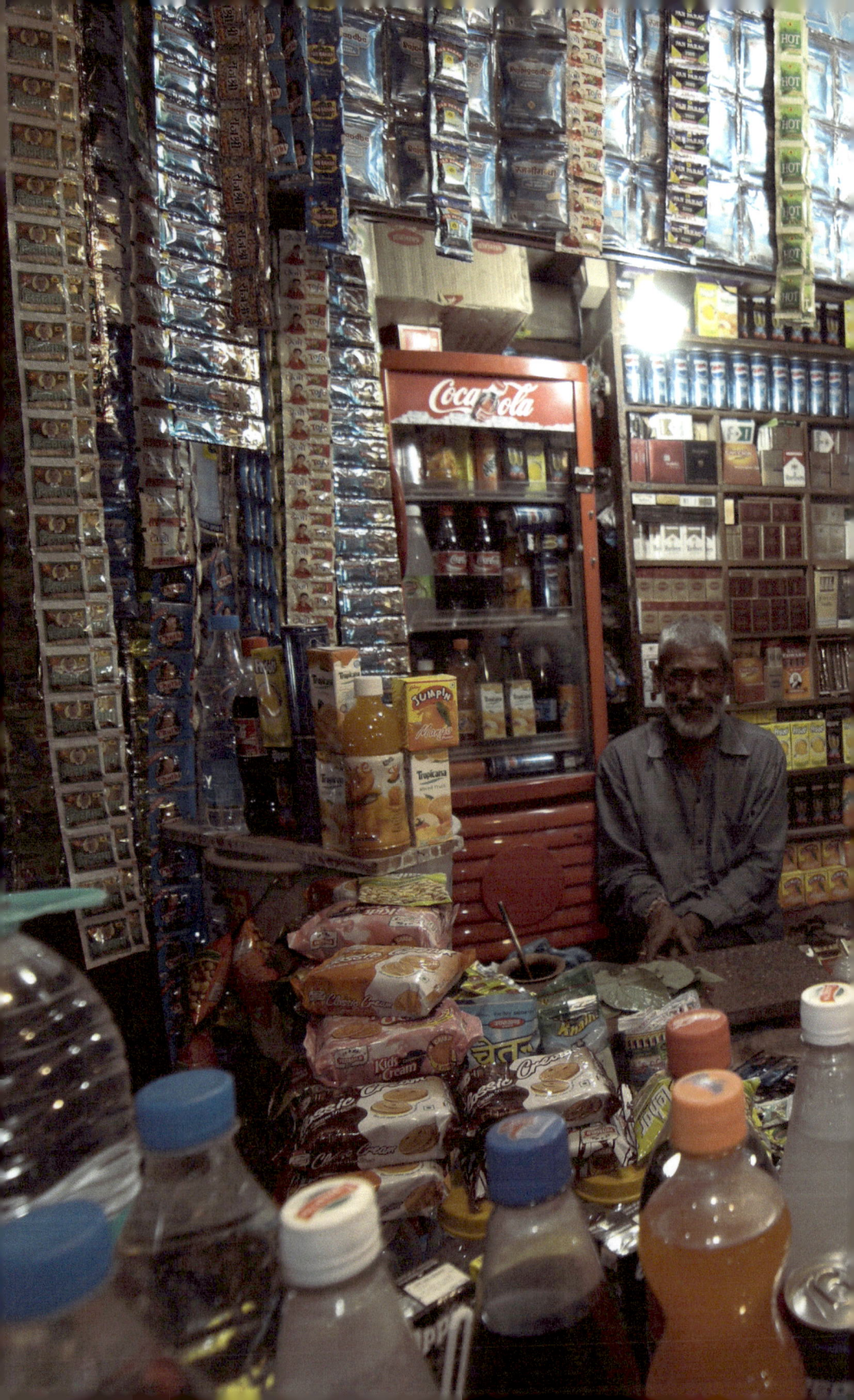

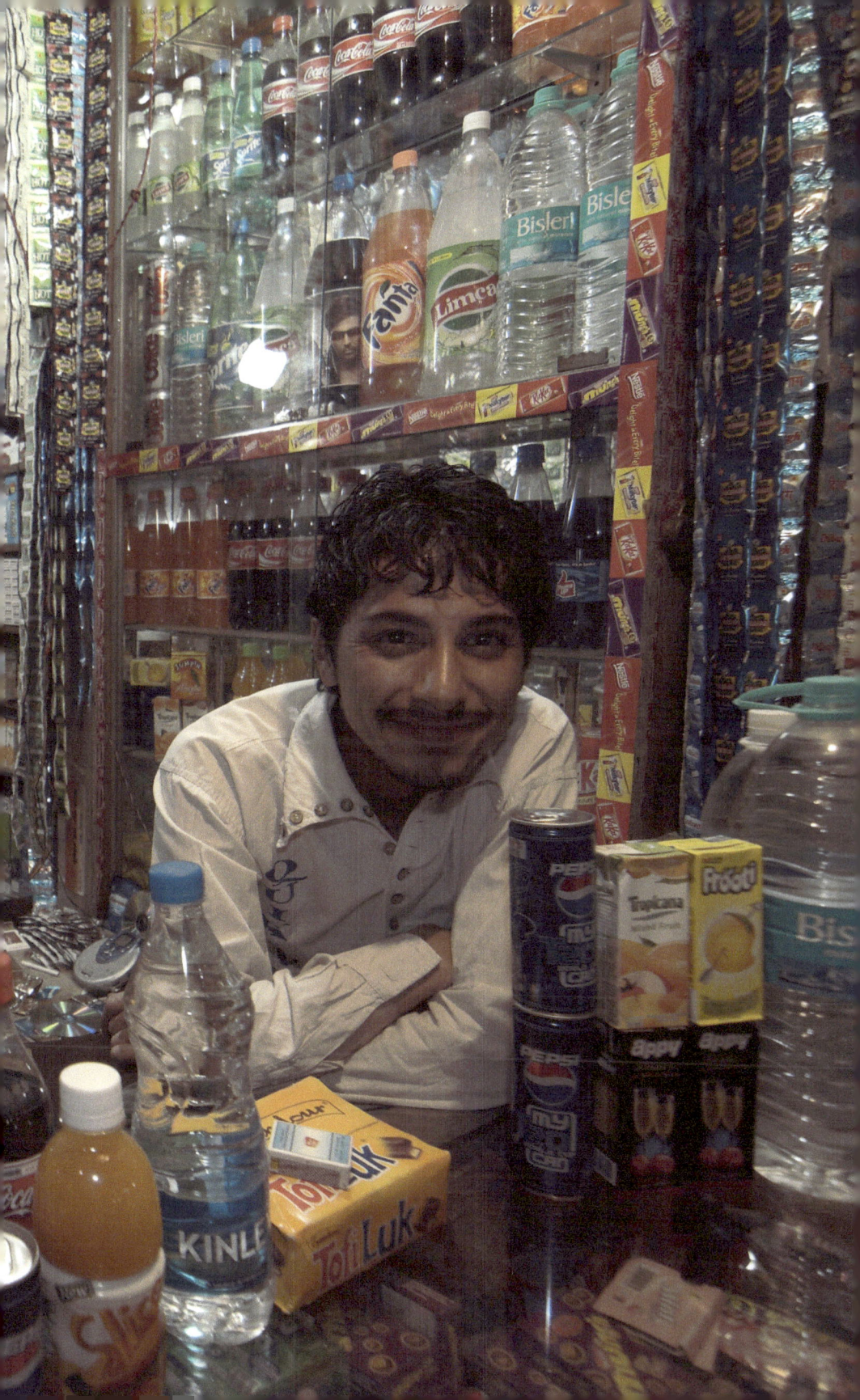

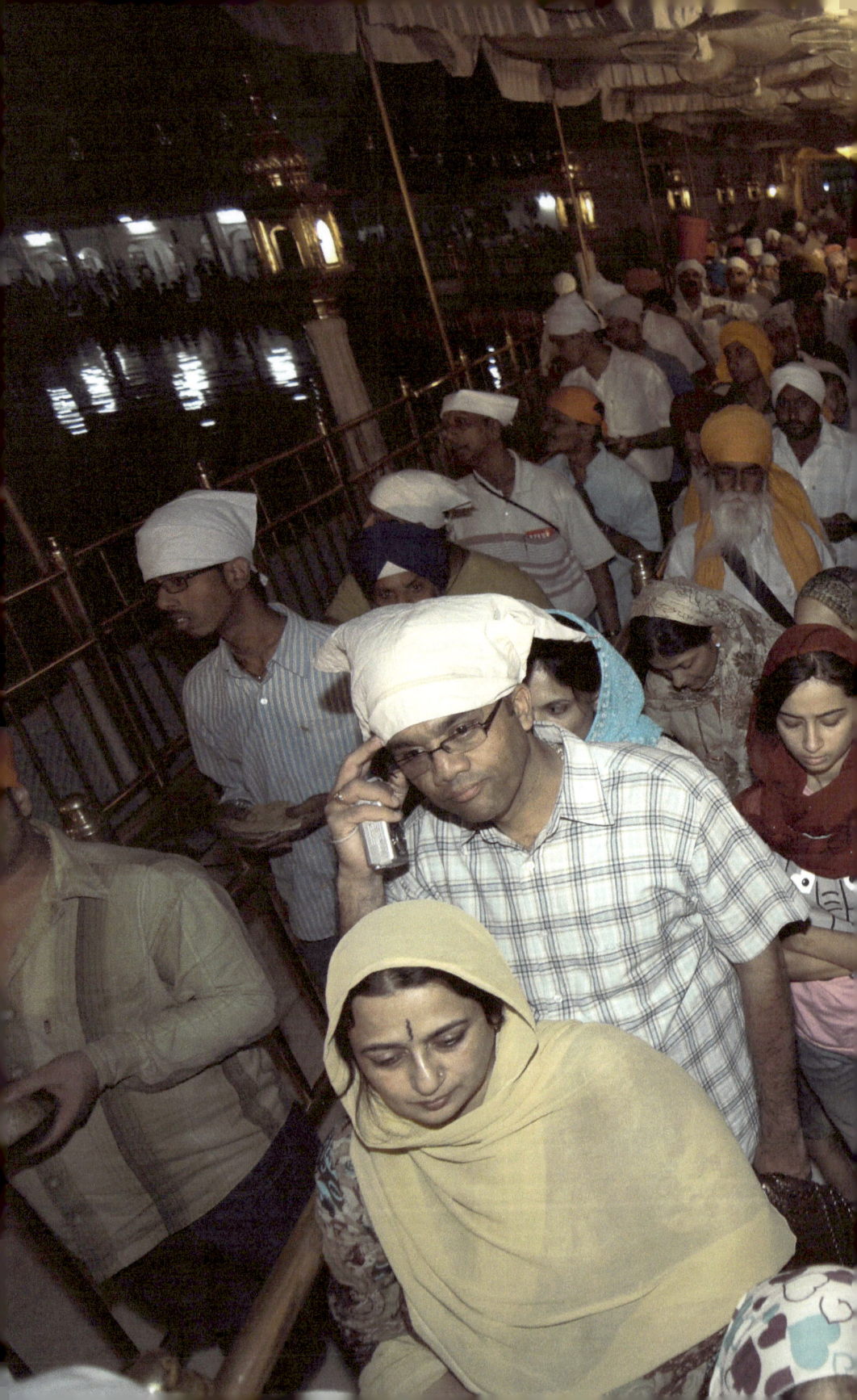

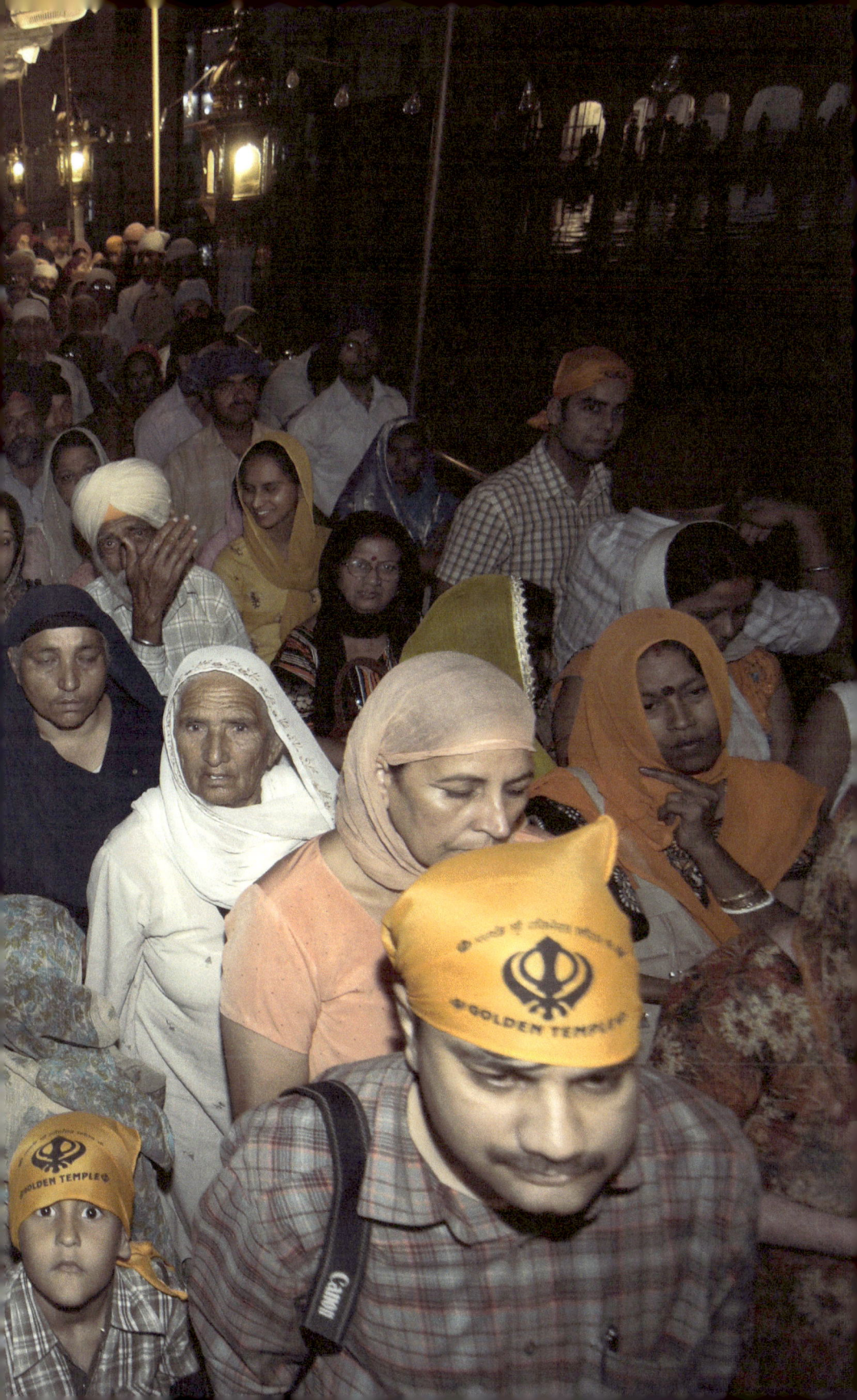

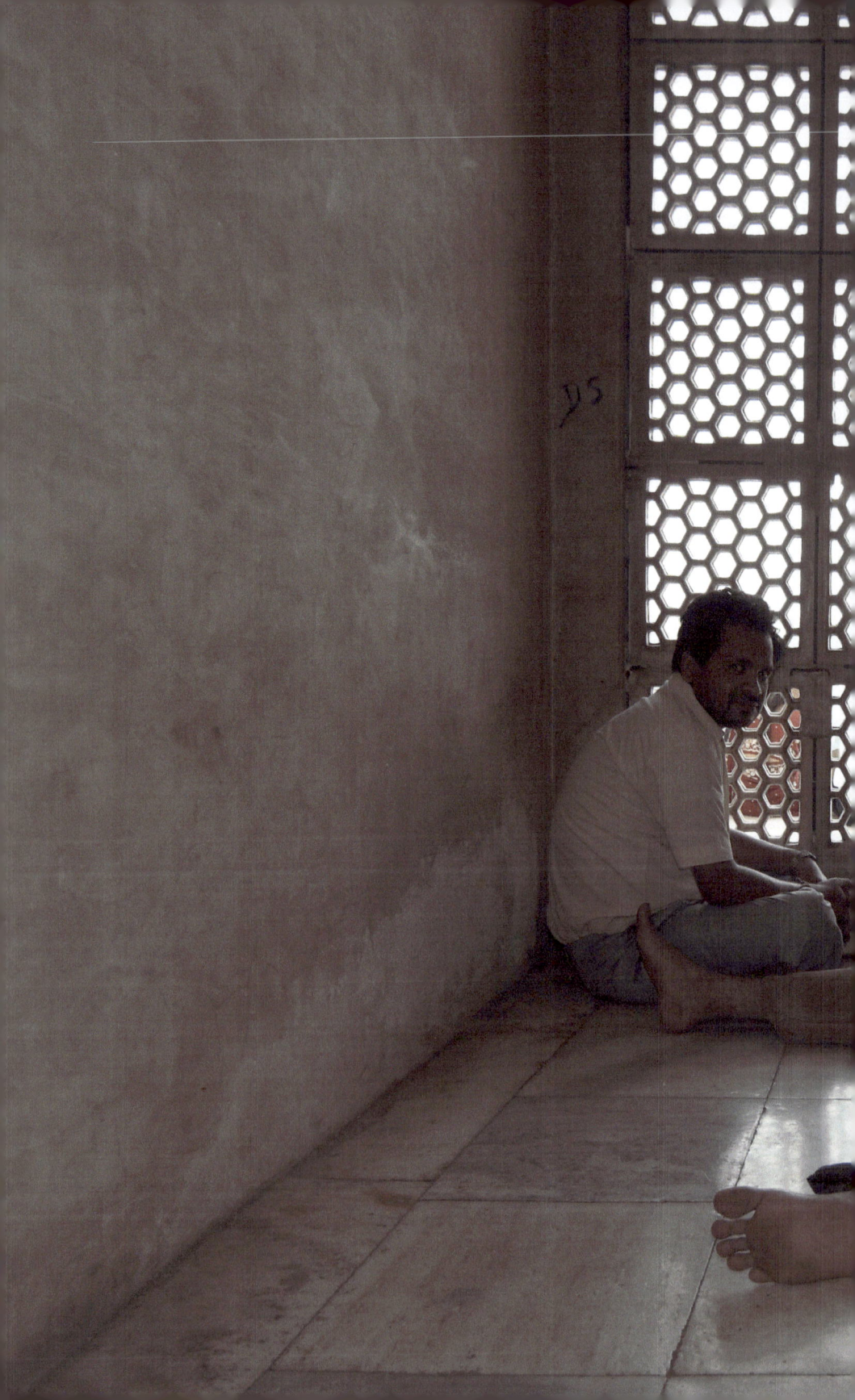

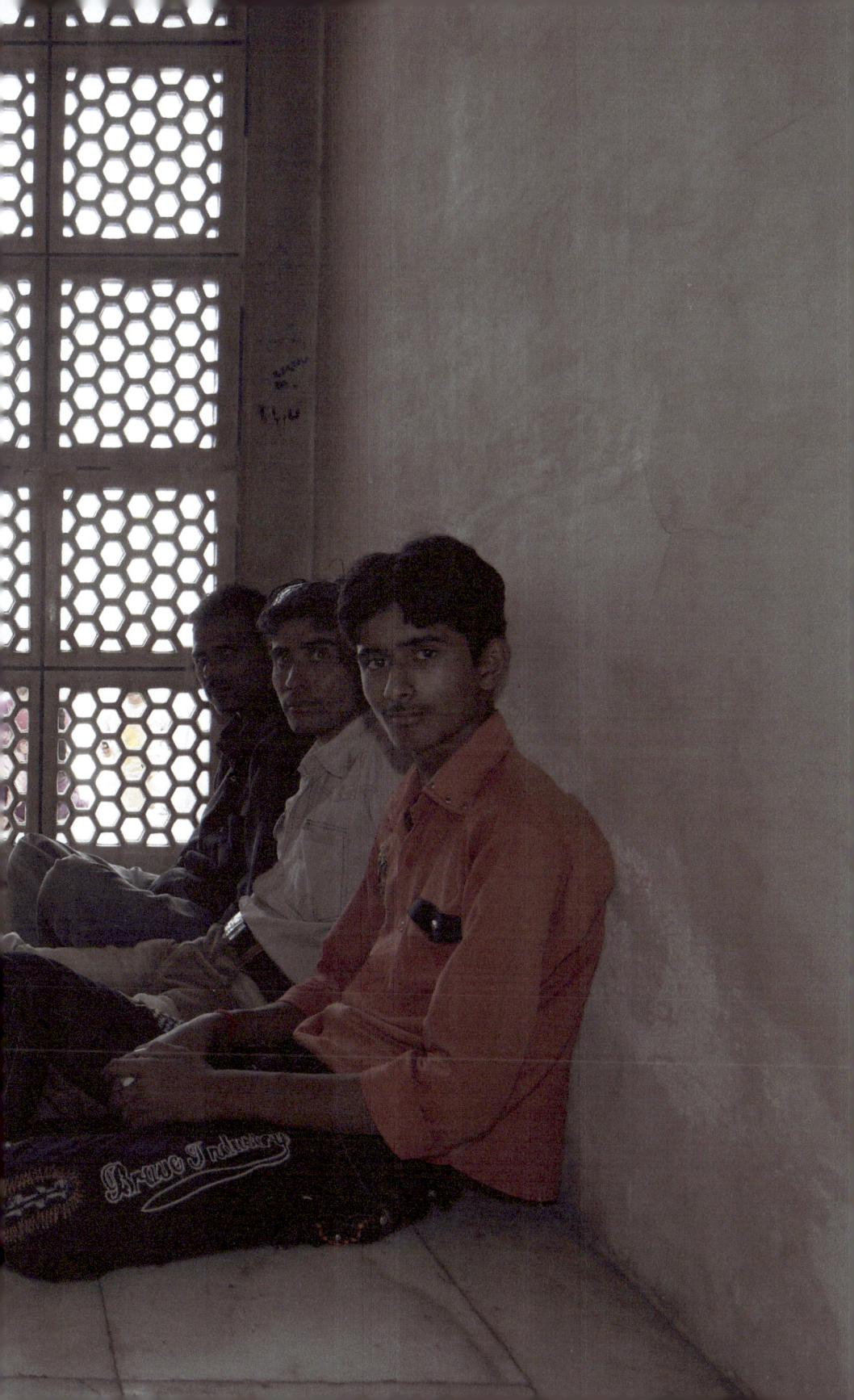

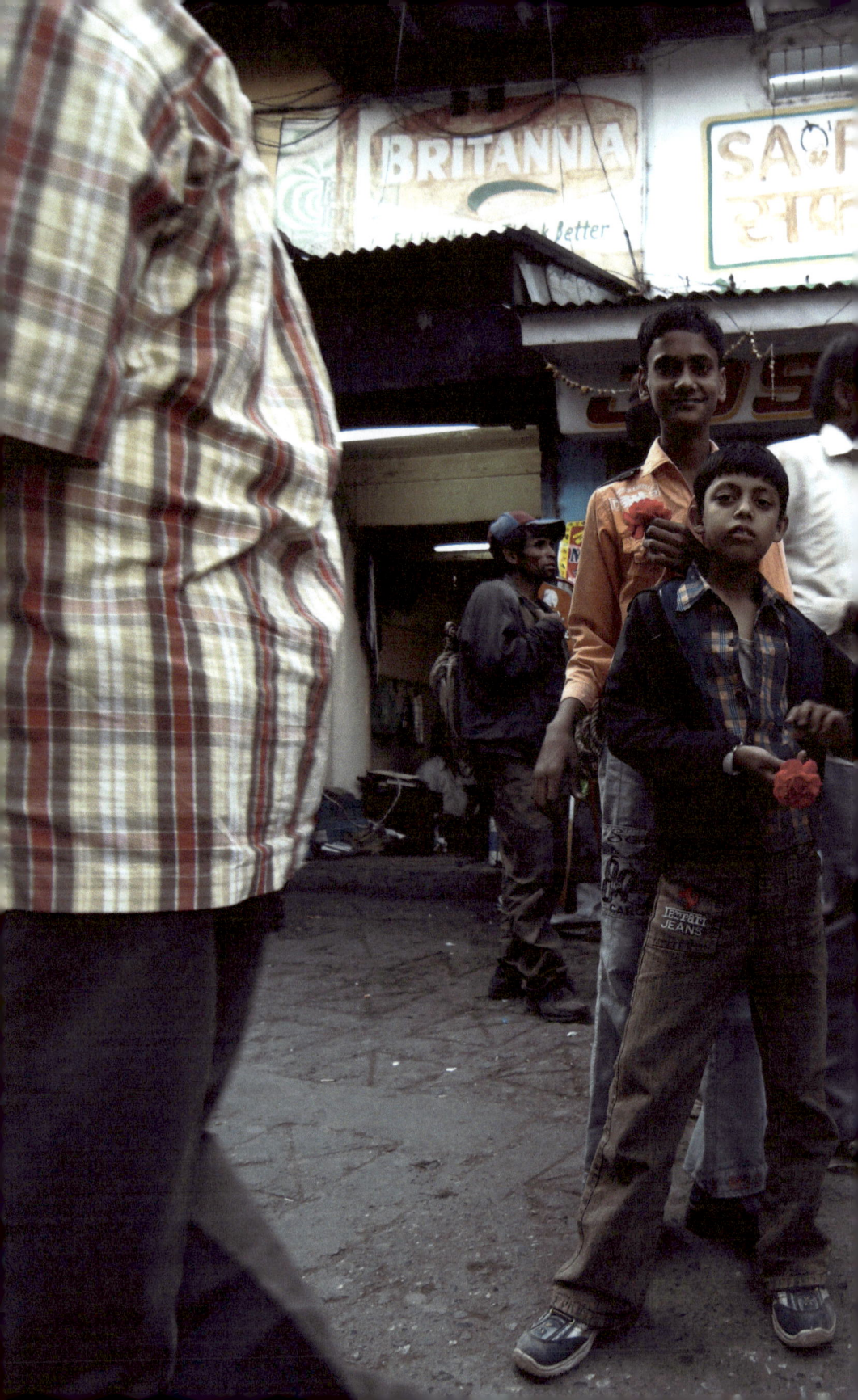

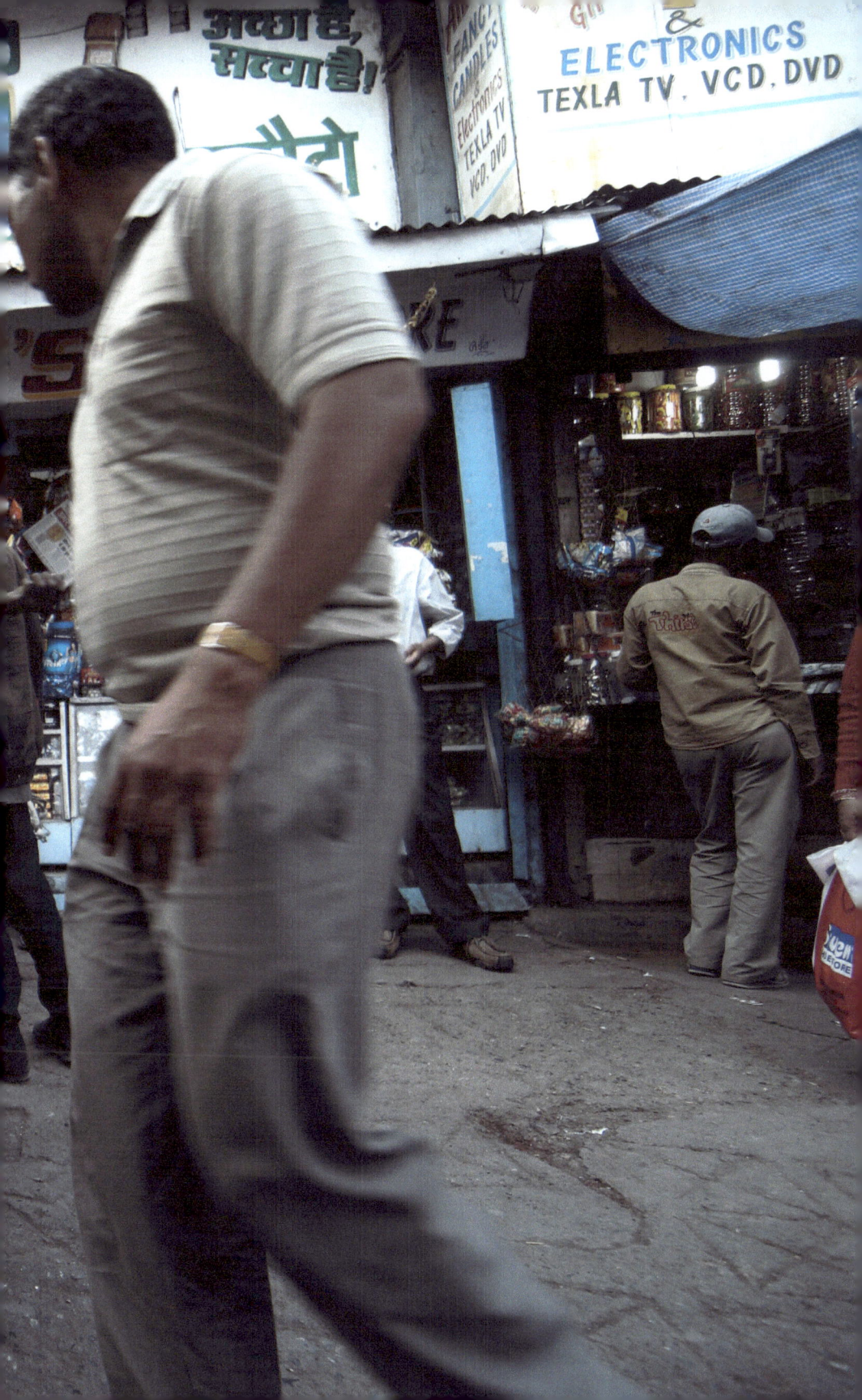

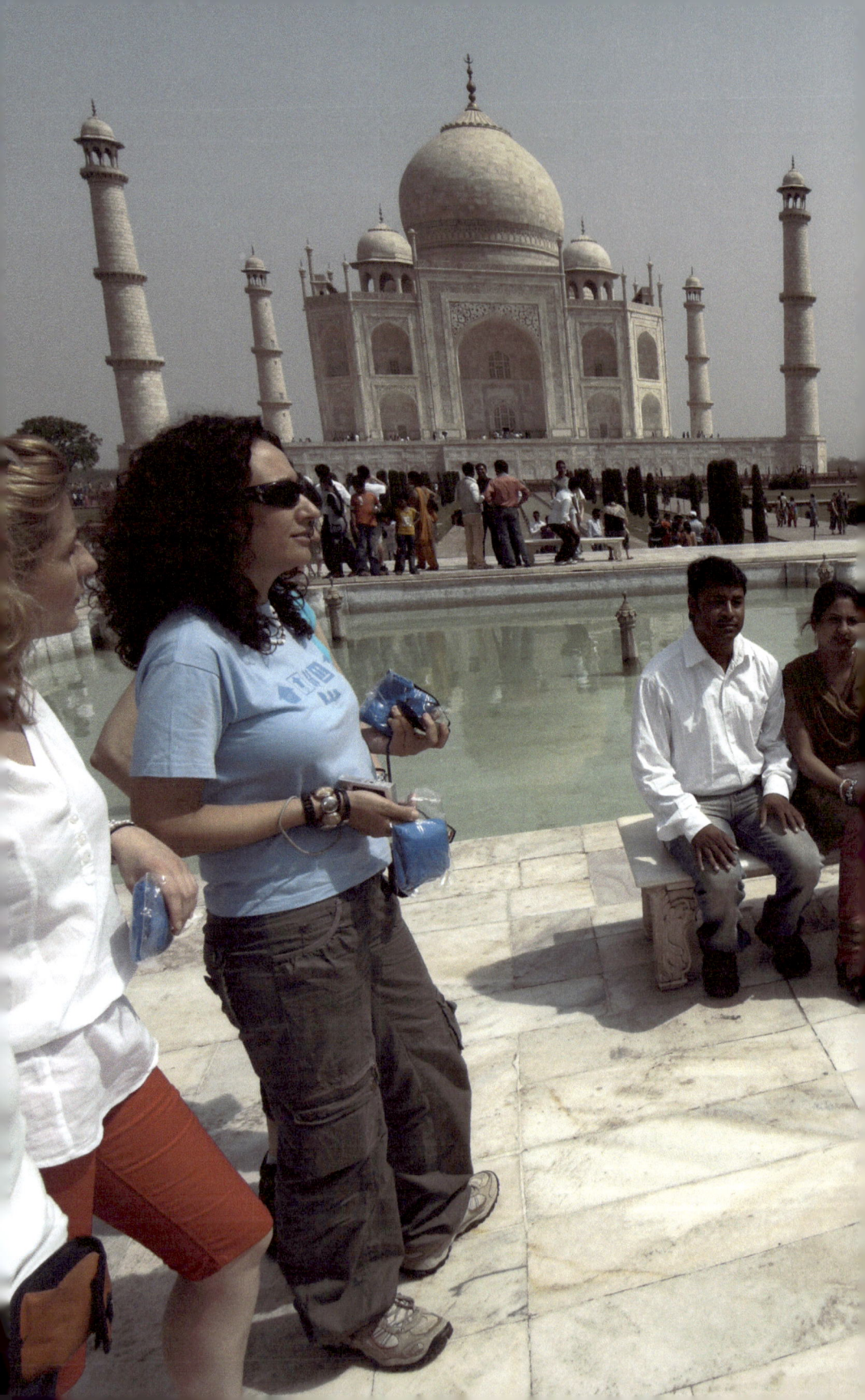

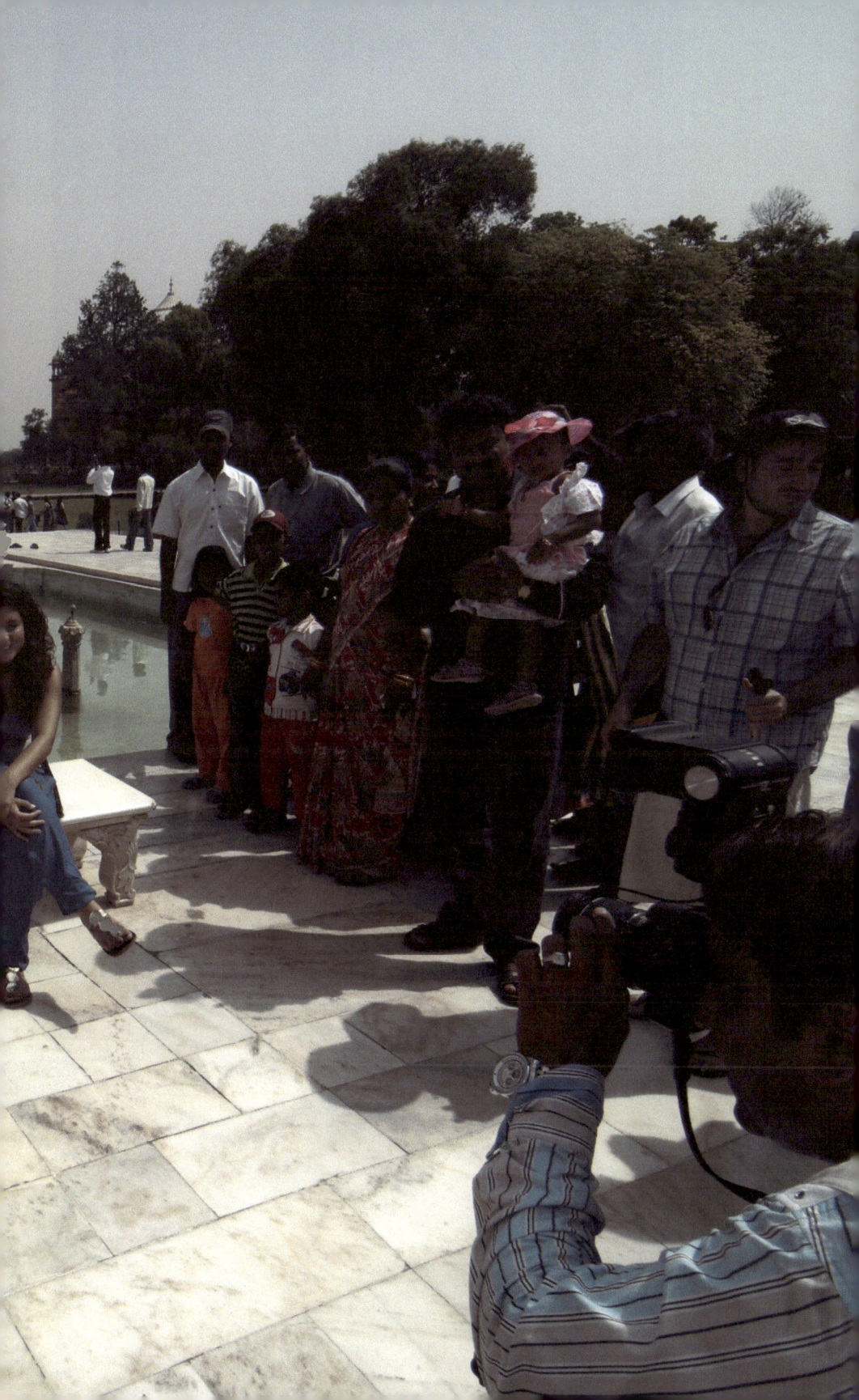

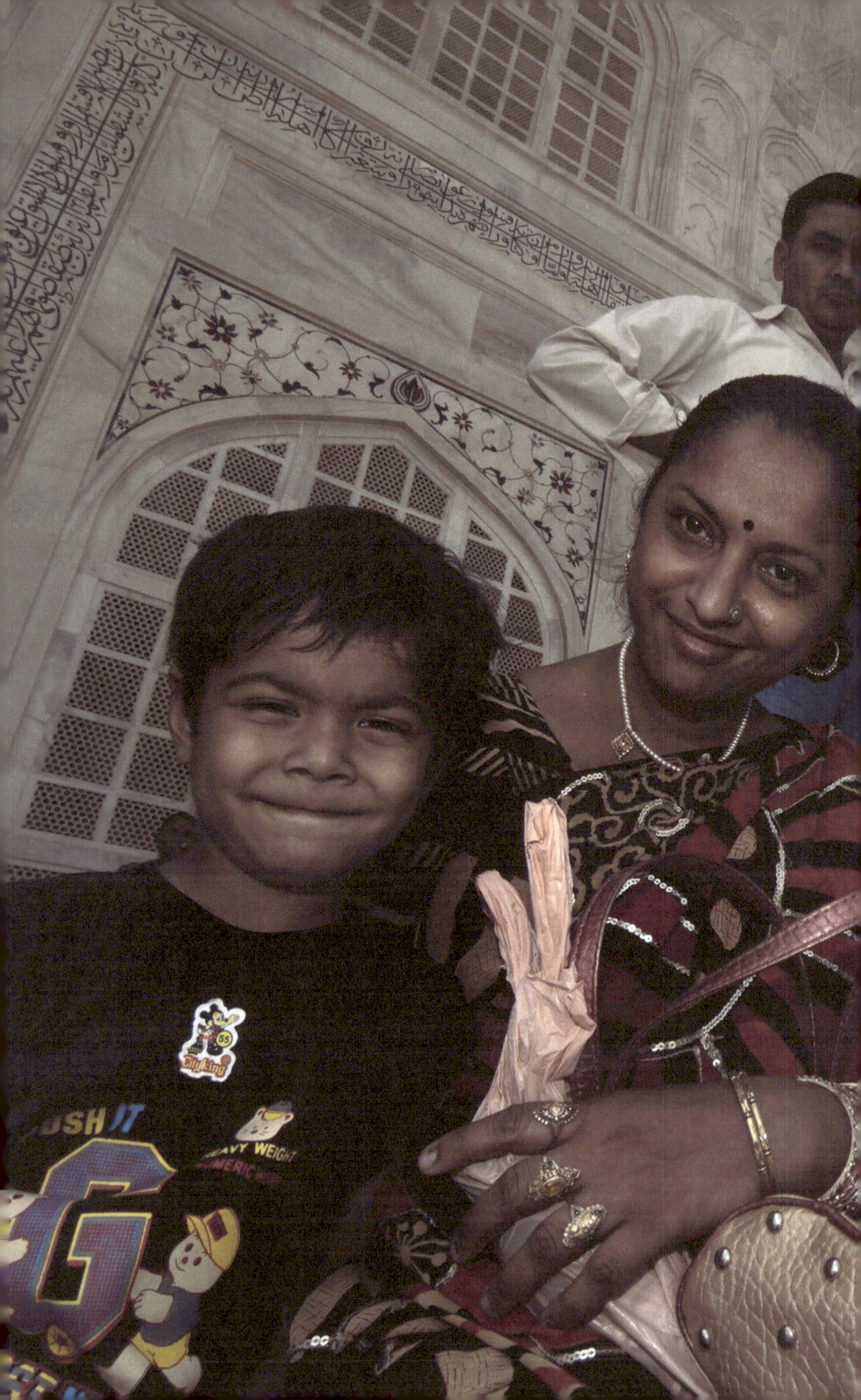

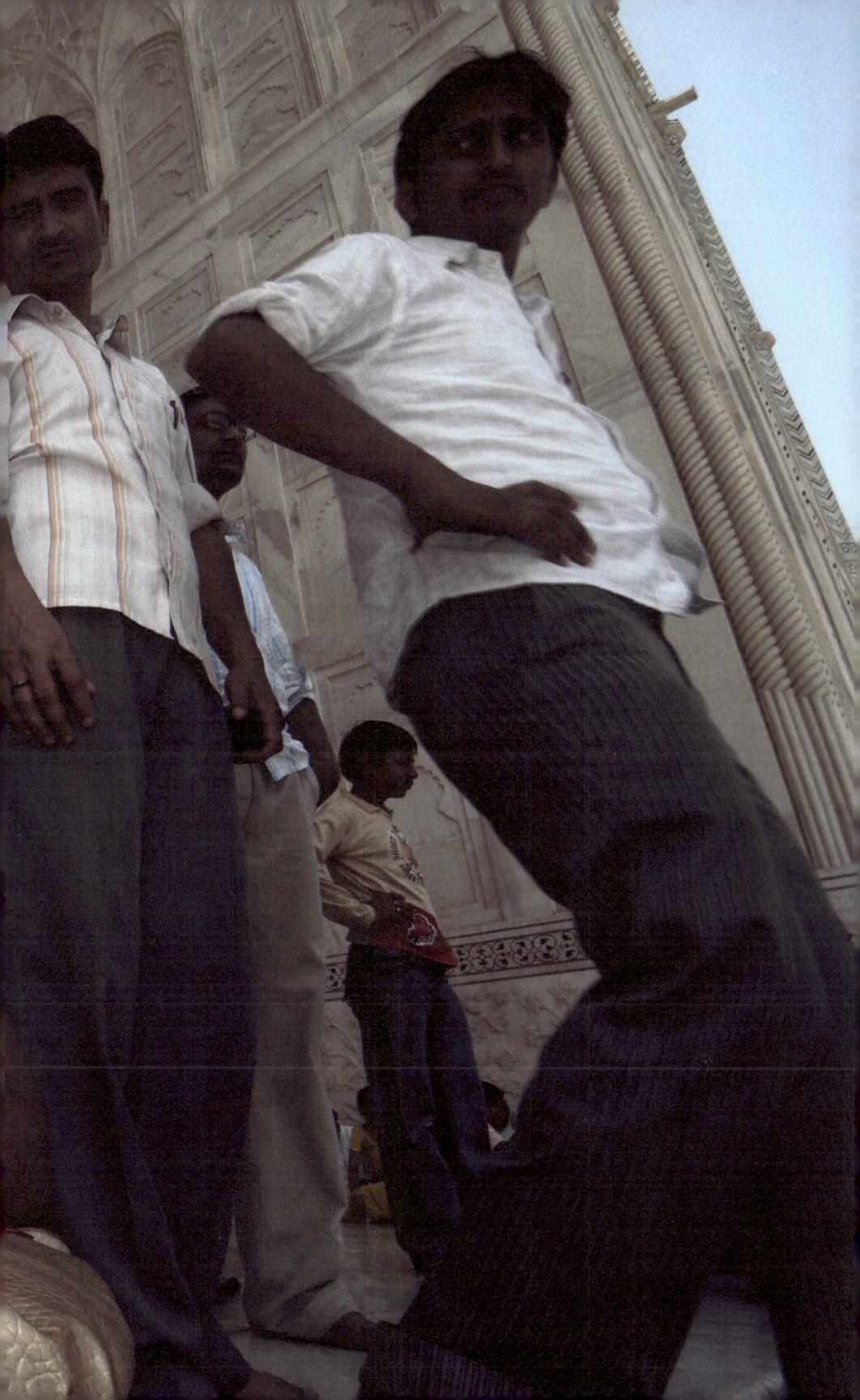

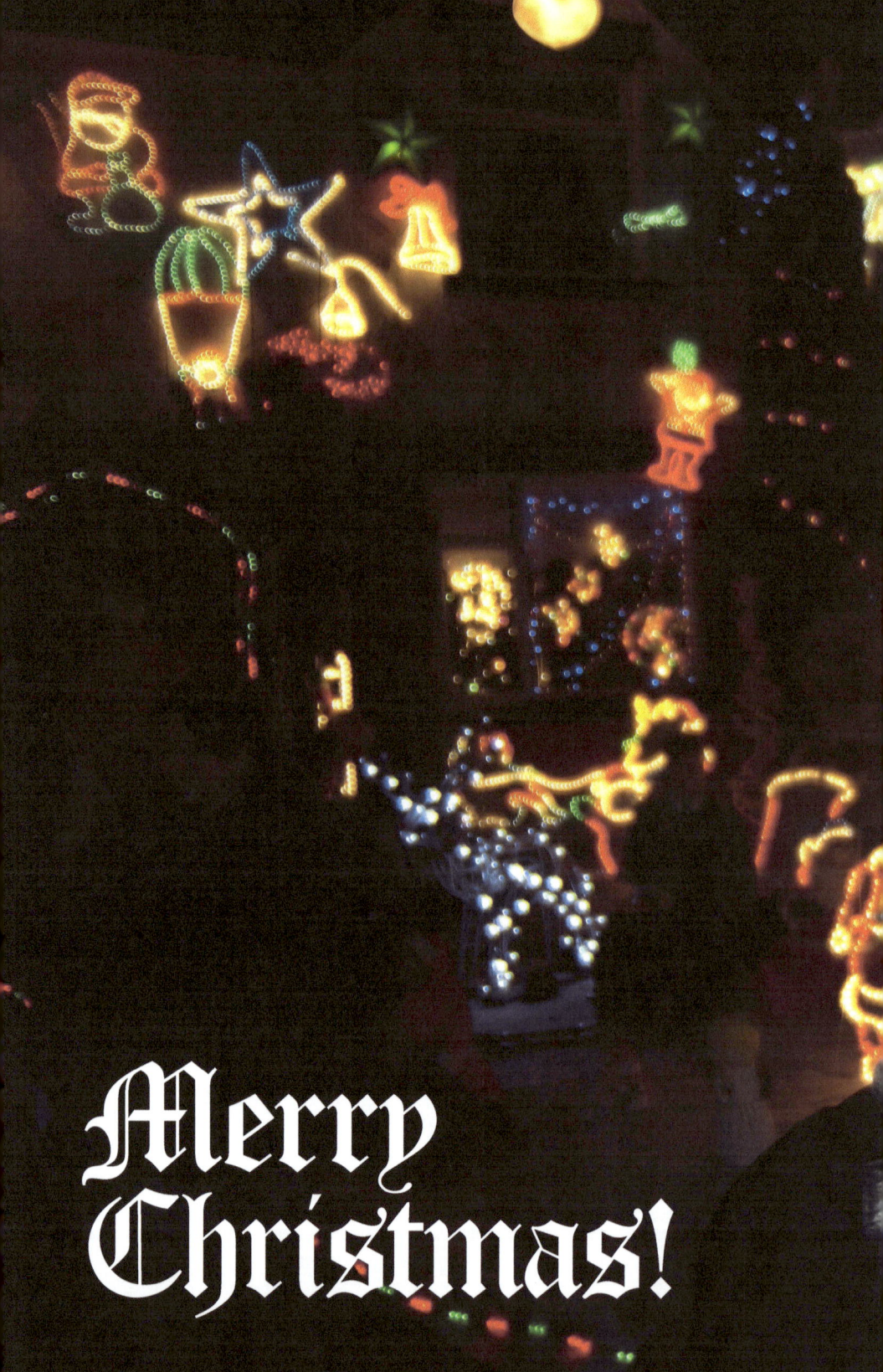

Merry Christmas!

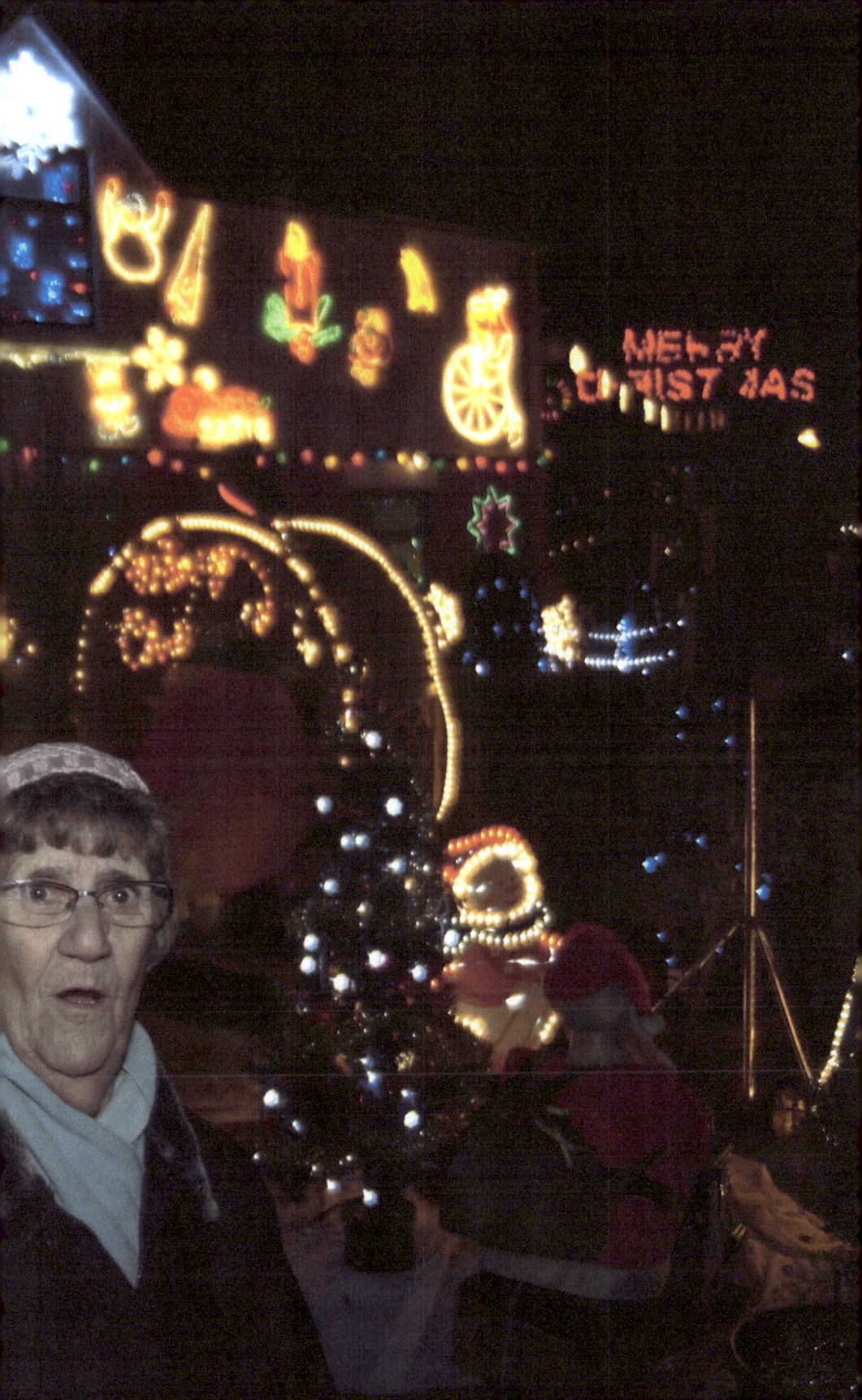

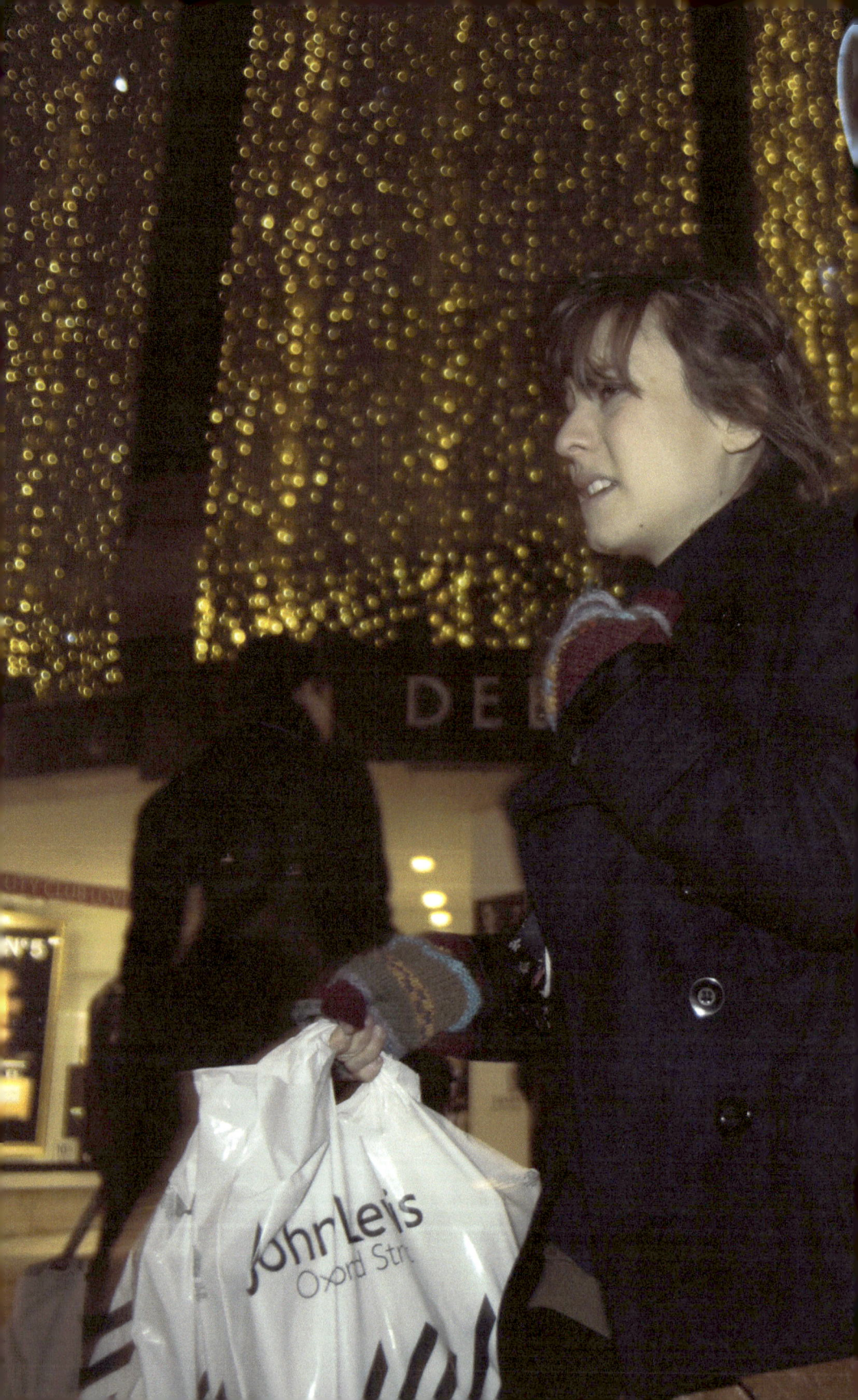

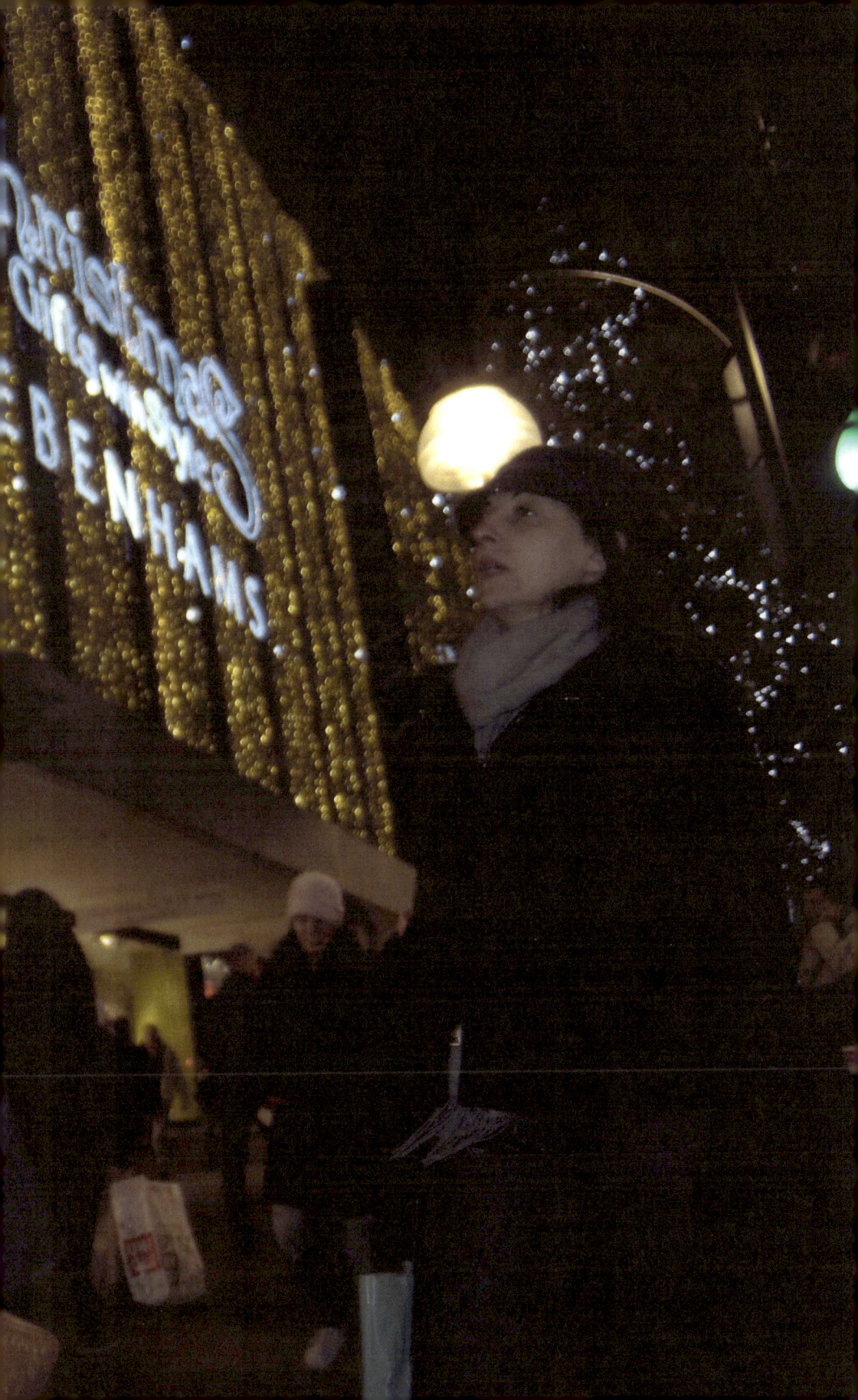

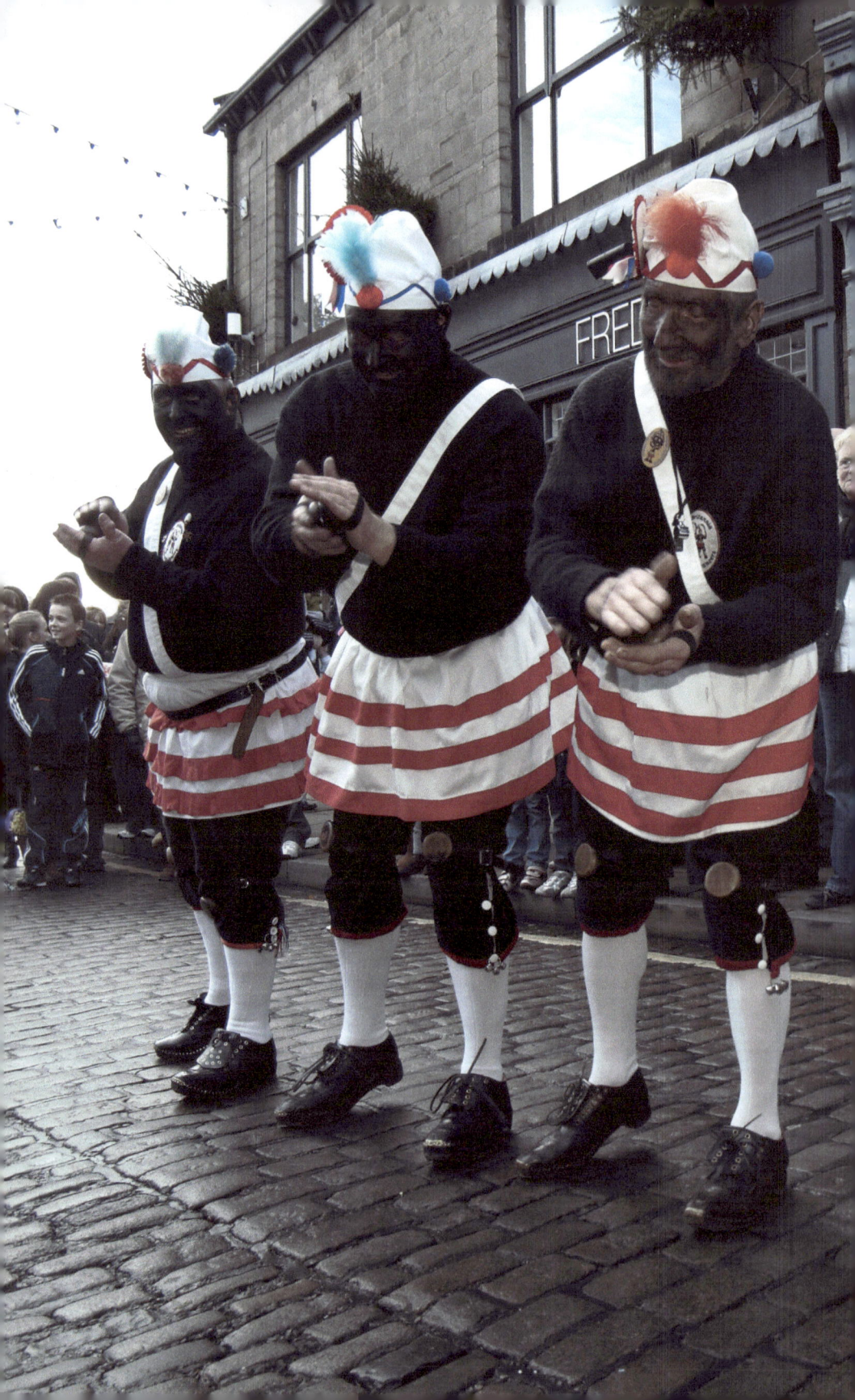

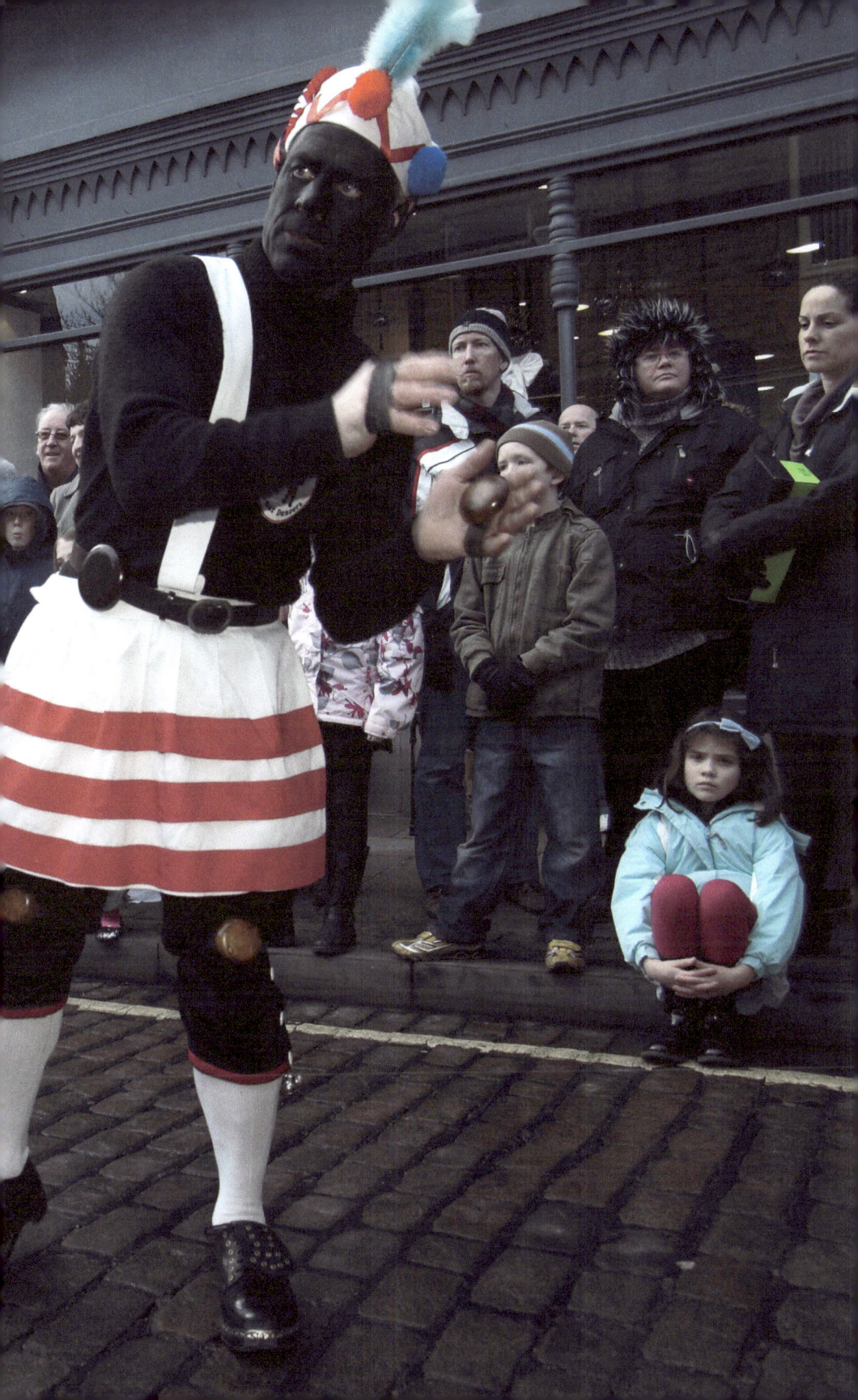

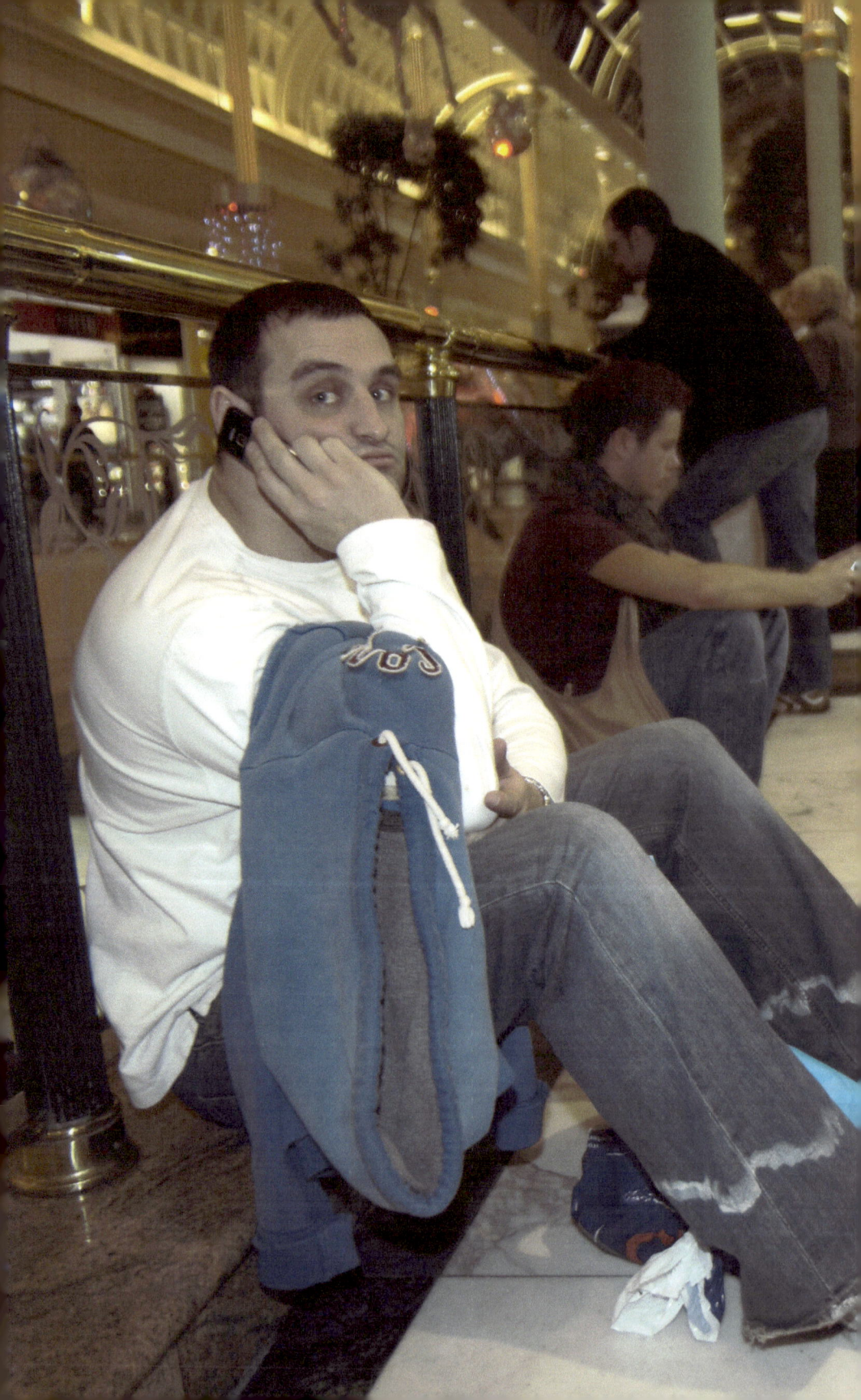

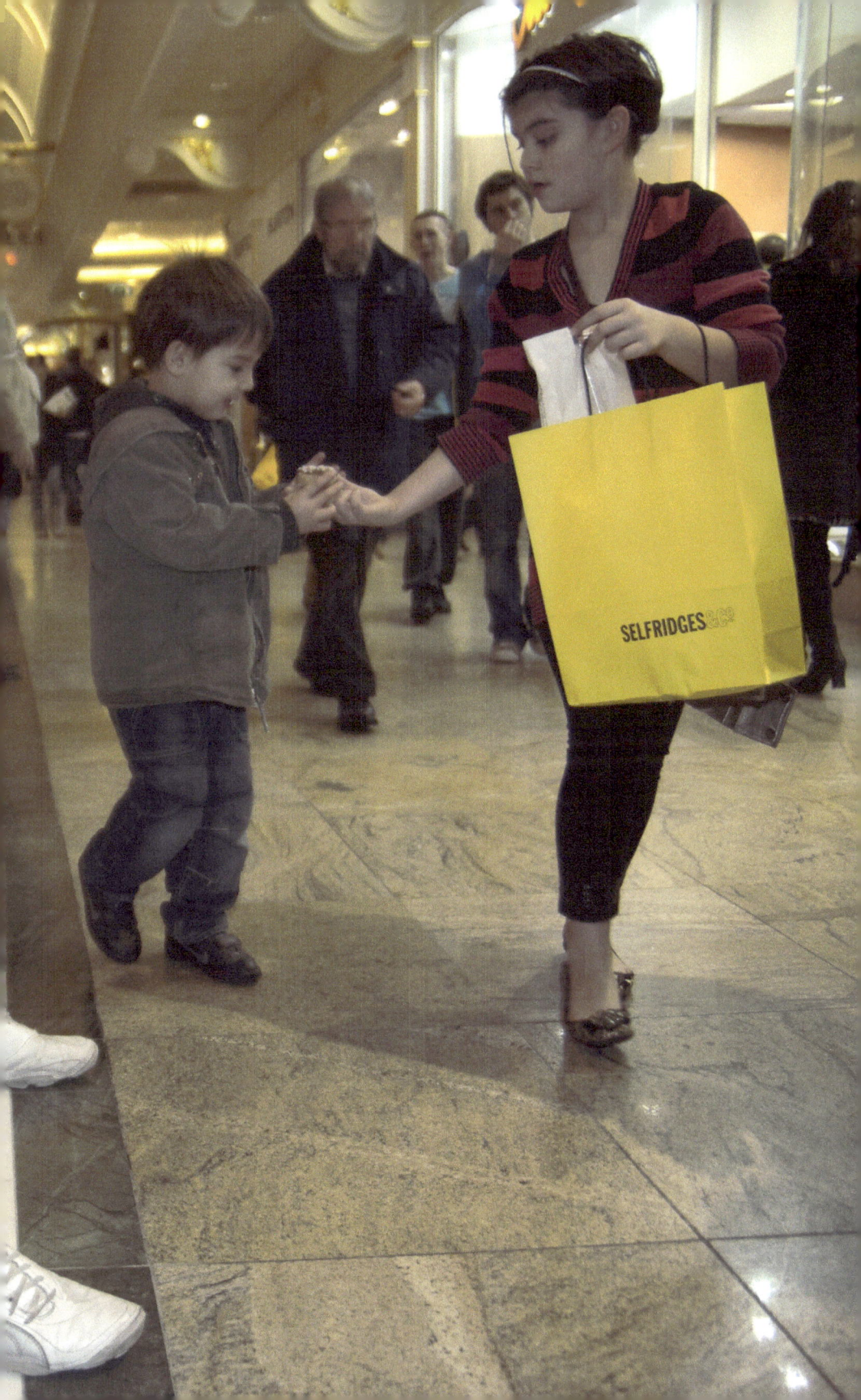

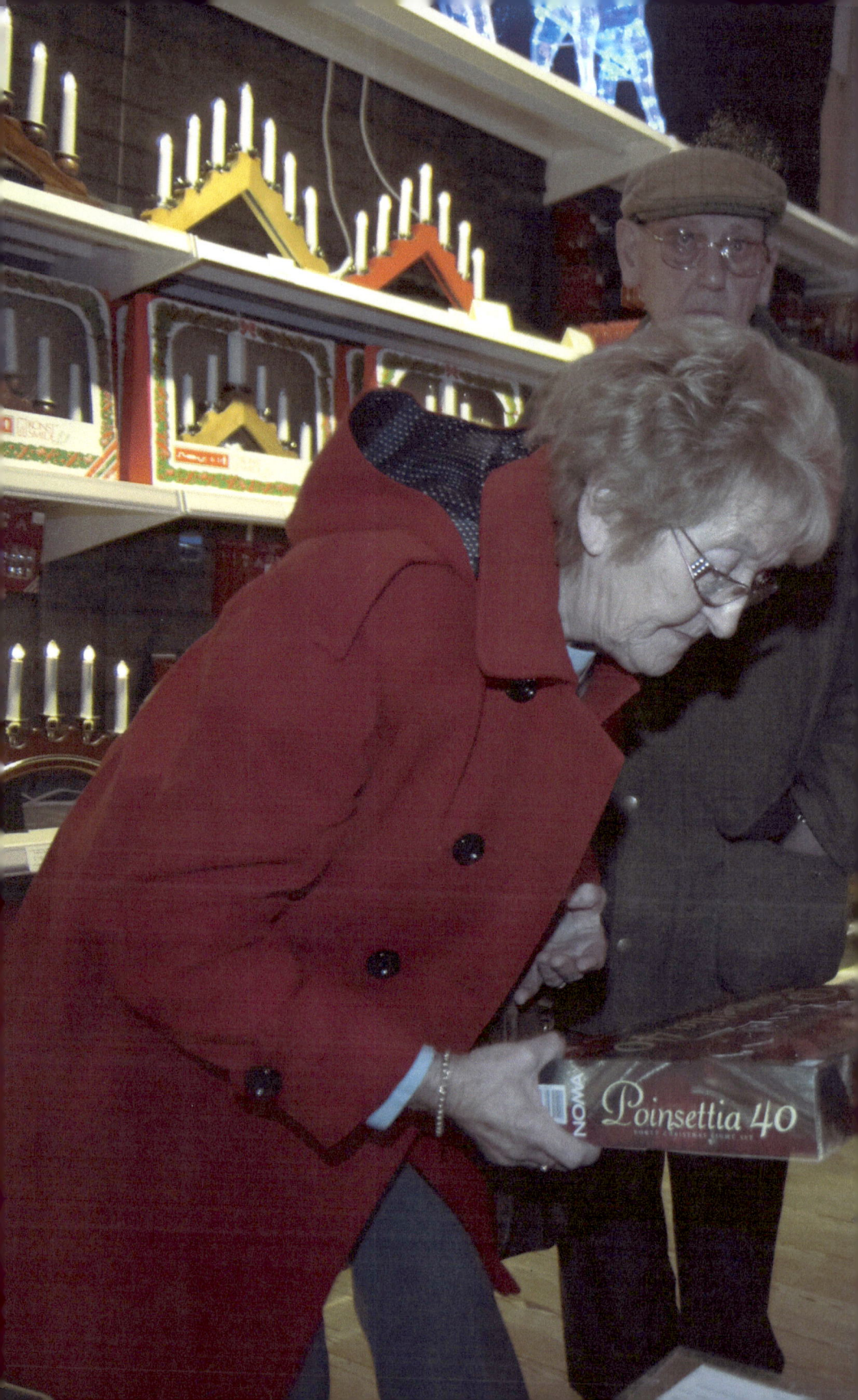

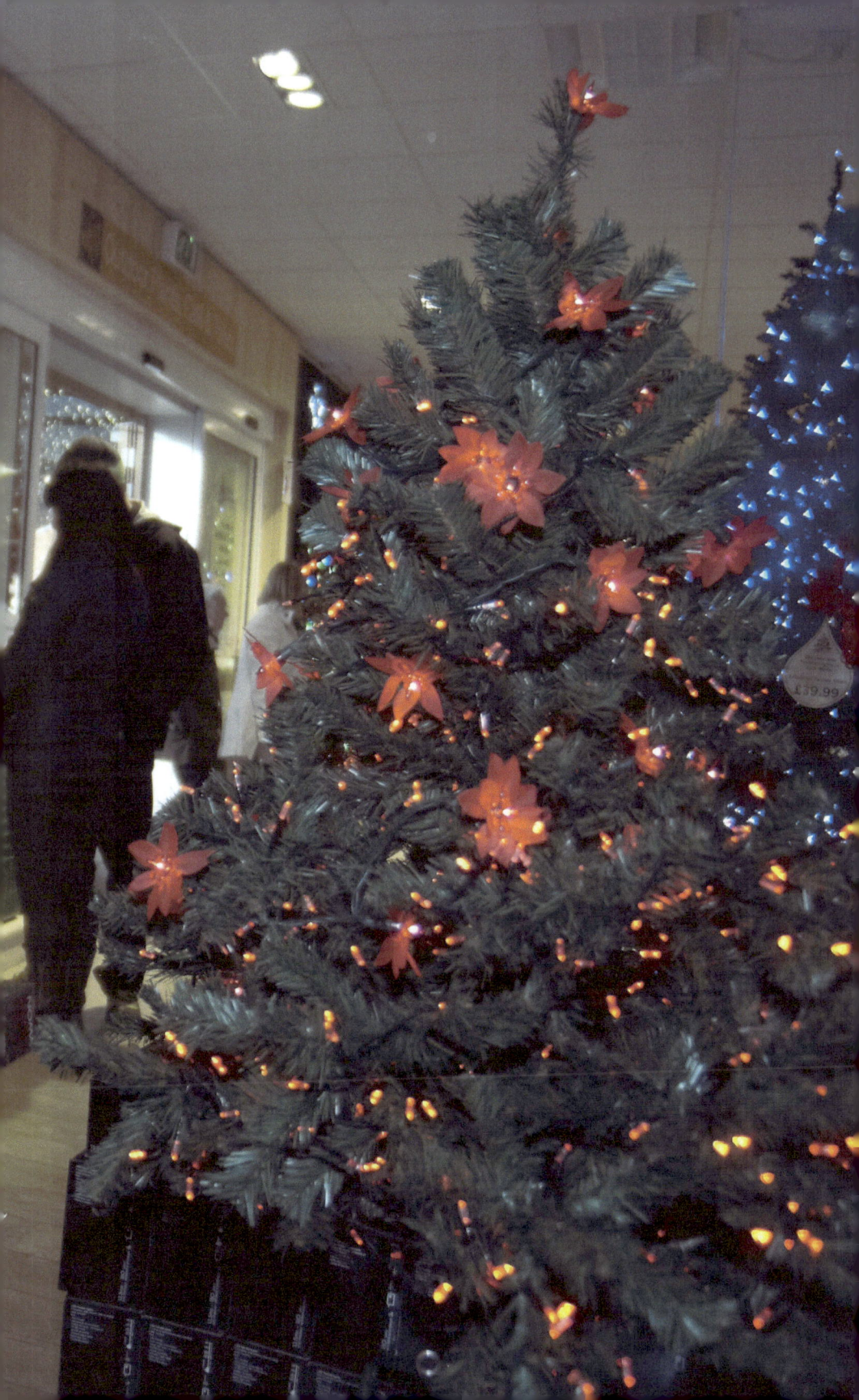

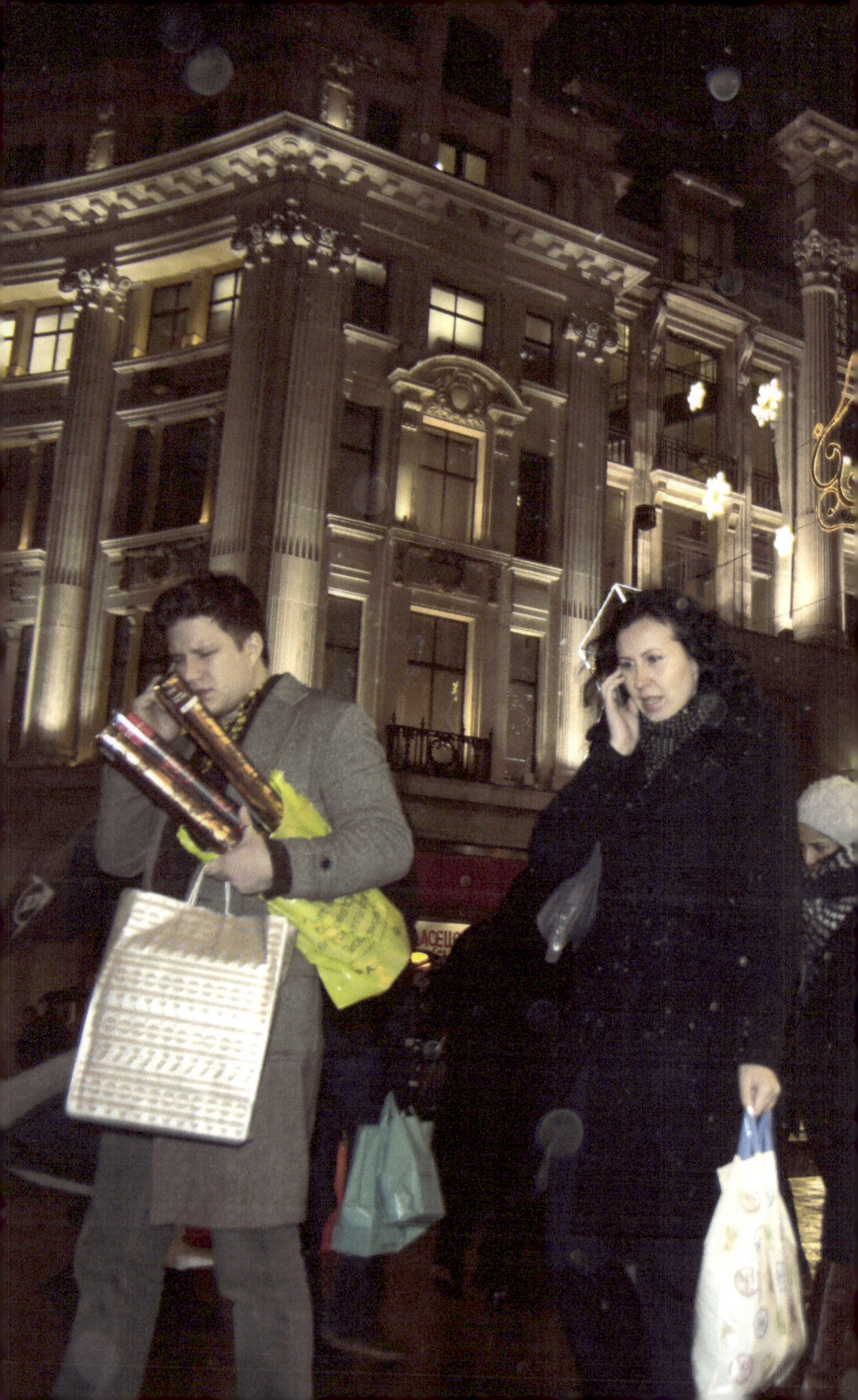

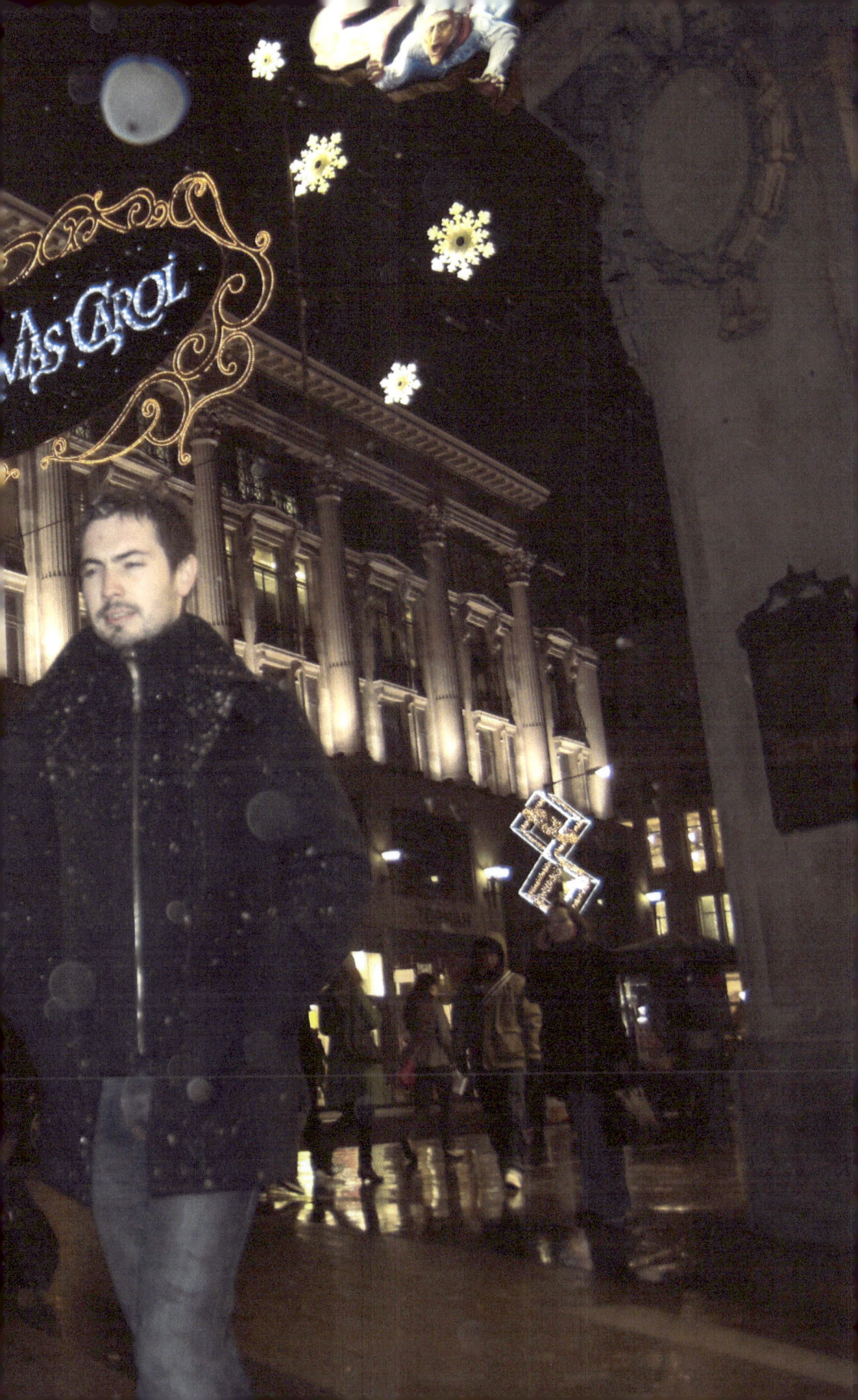

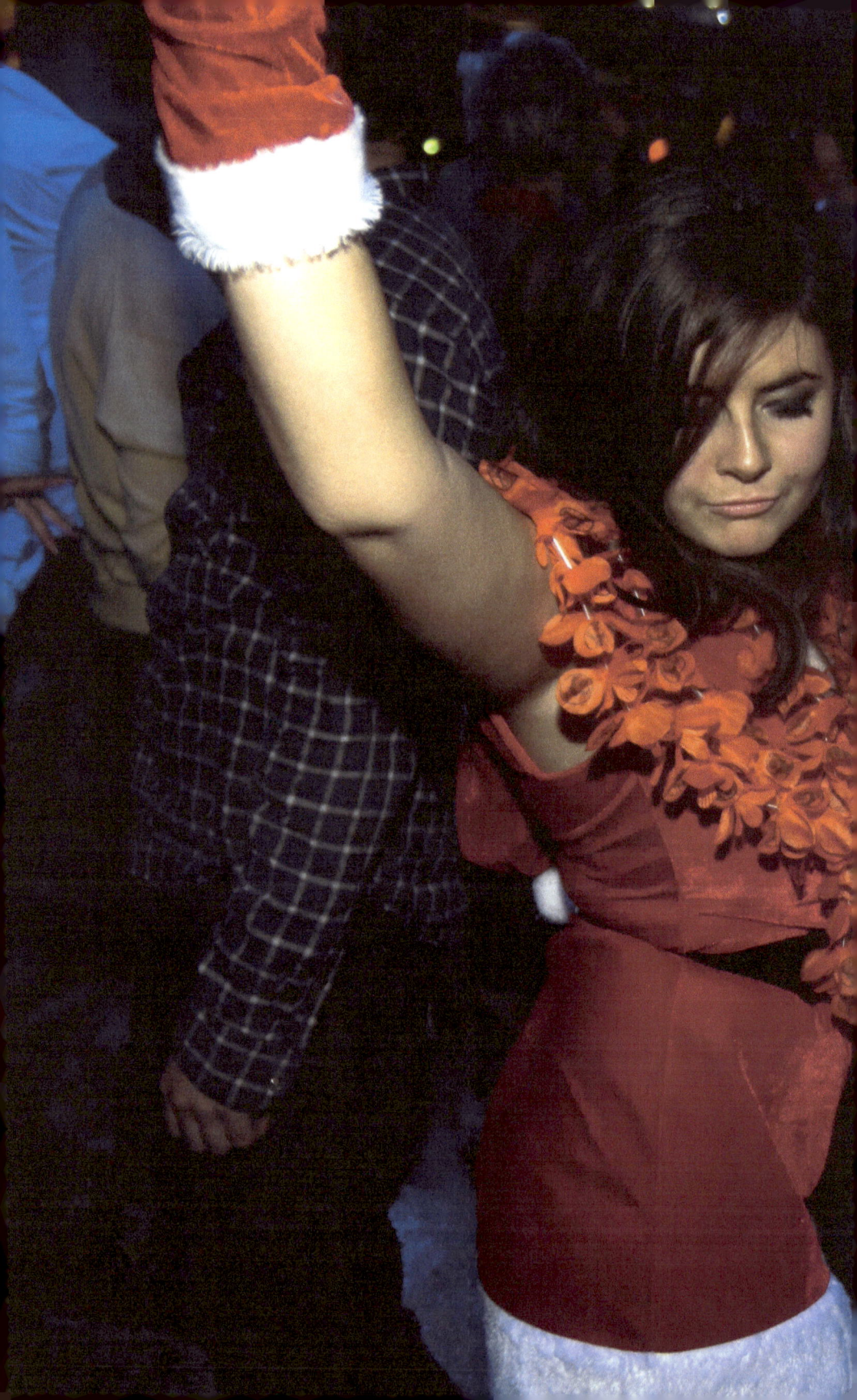

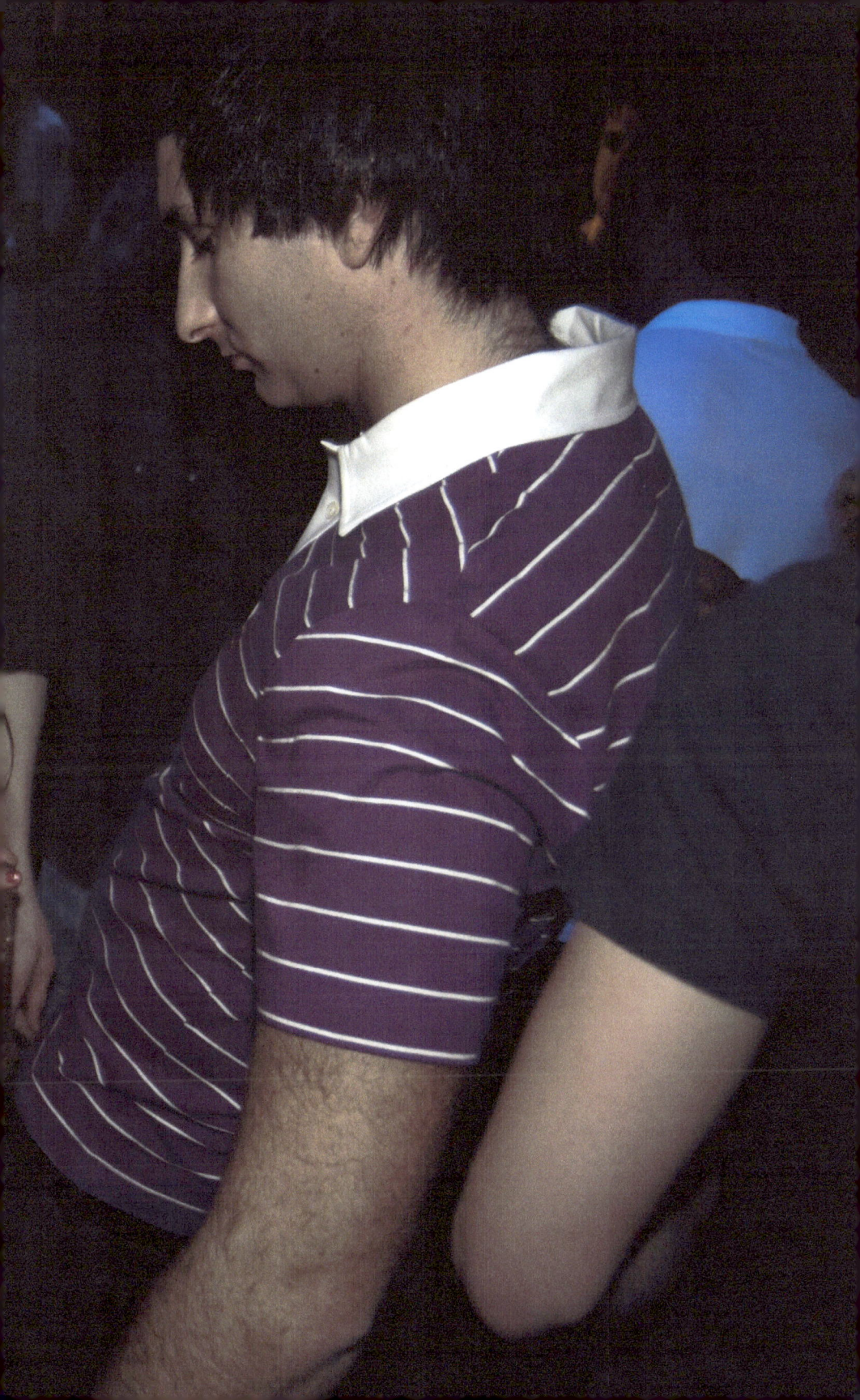

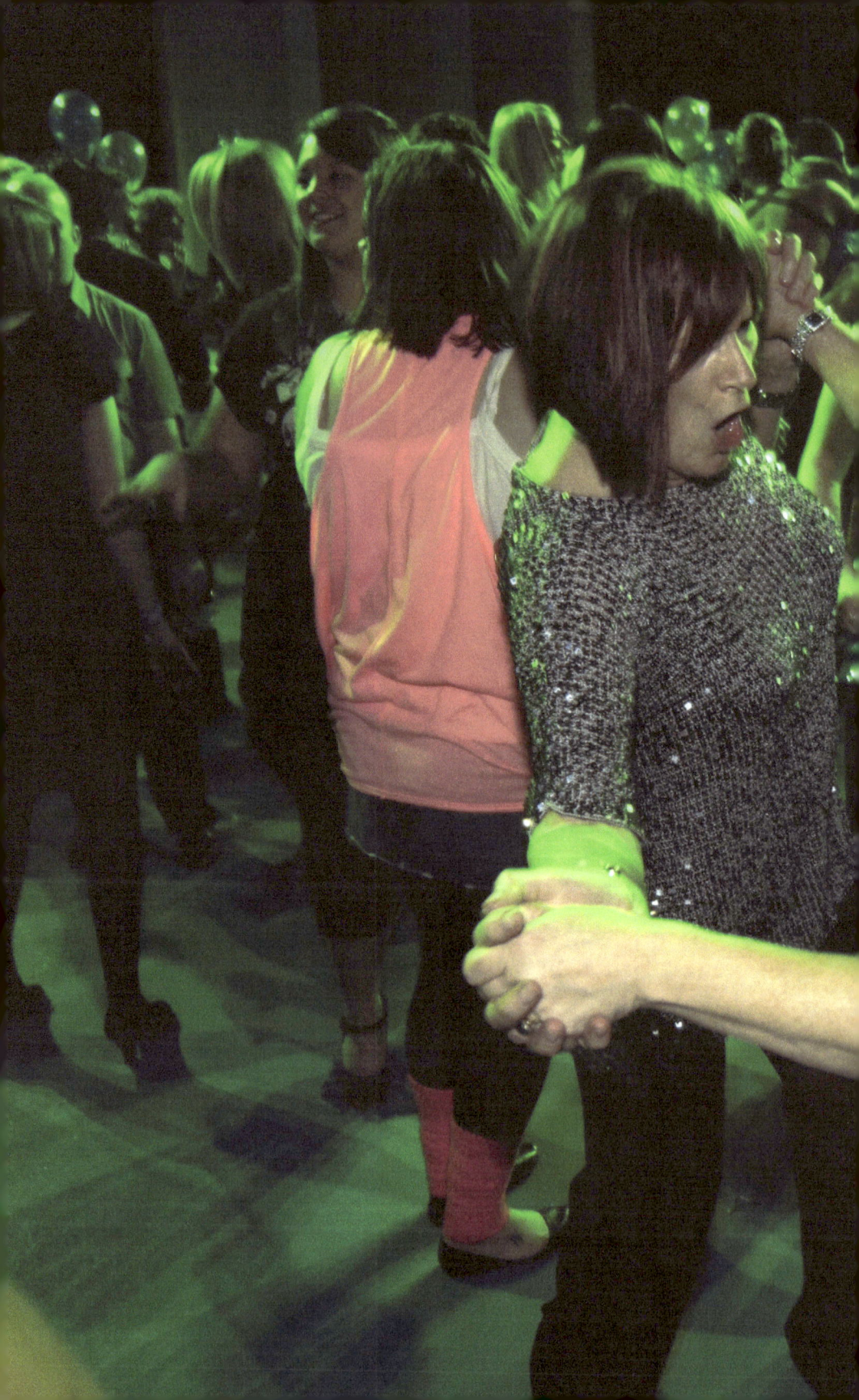

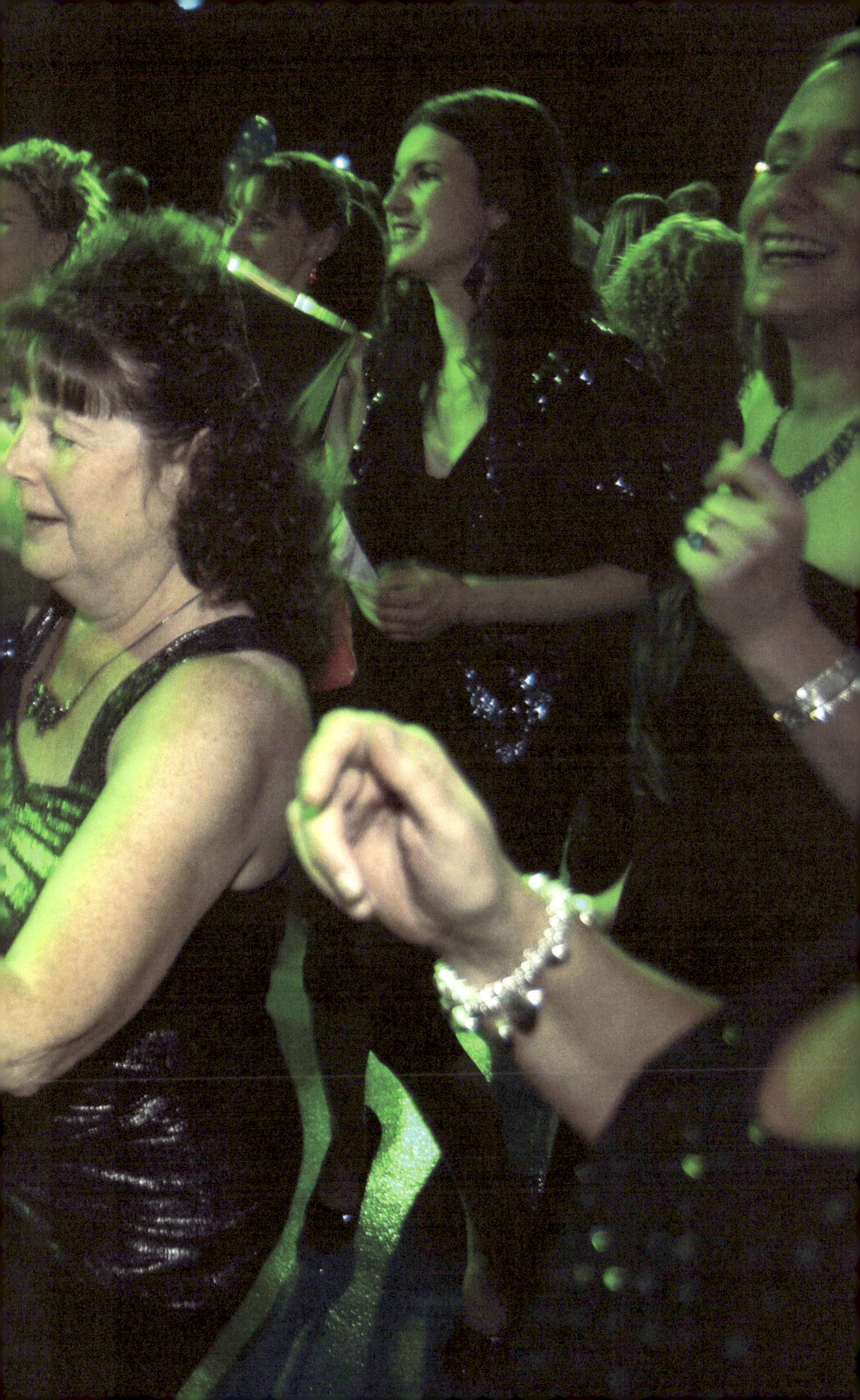

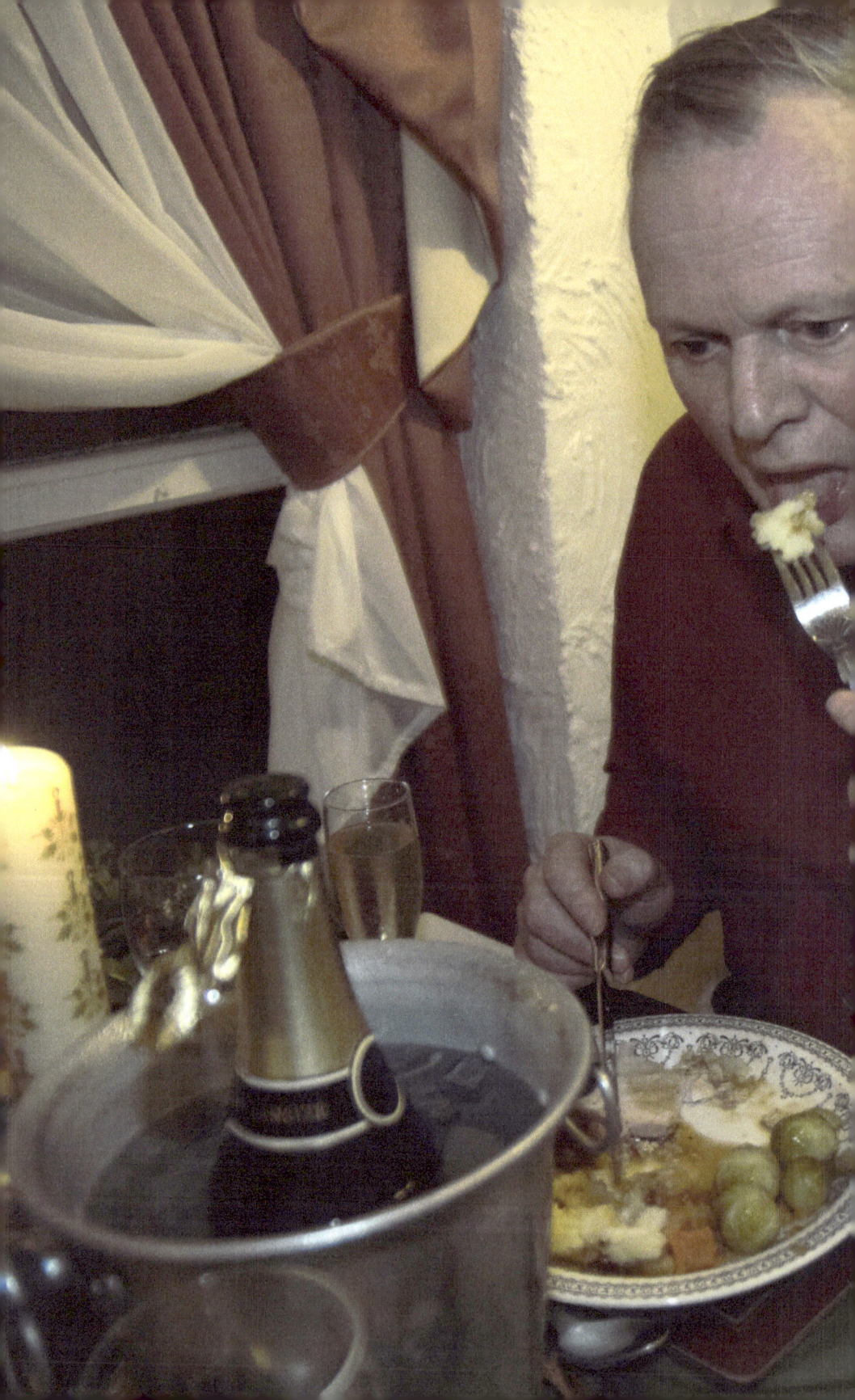

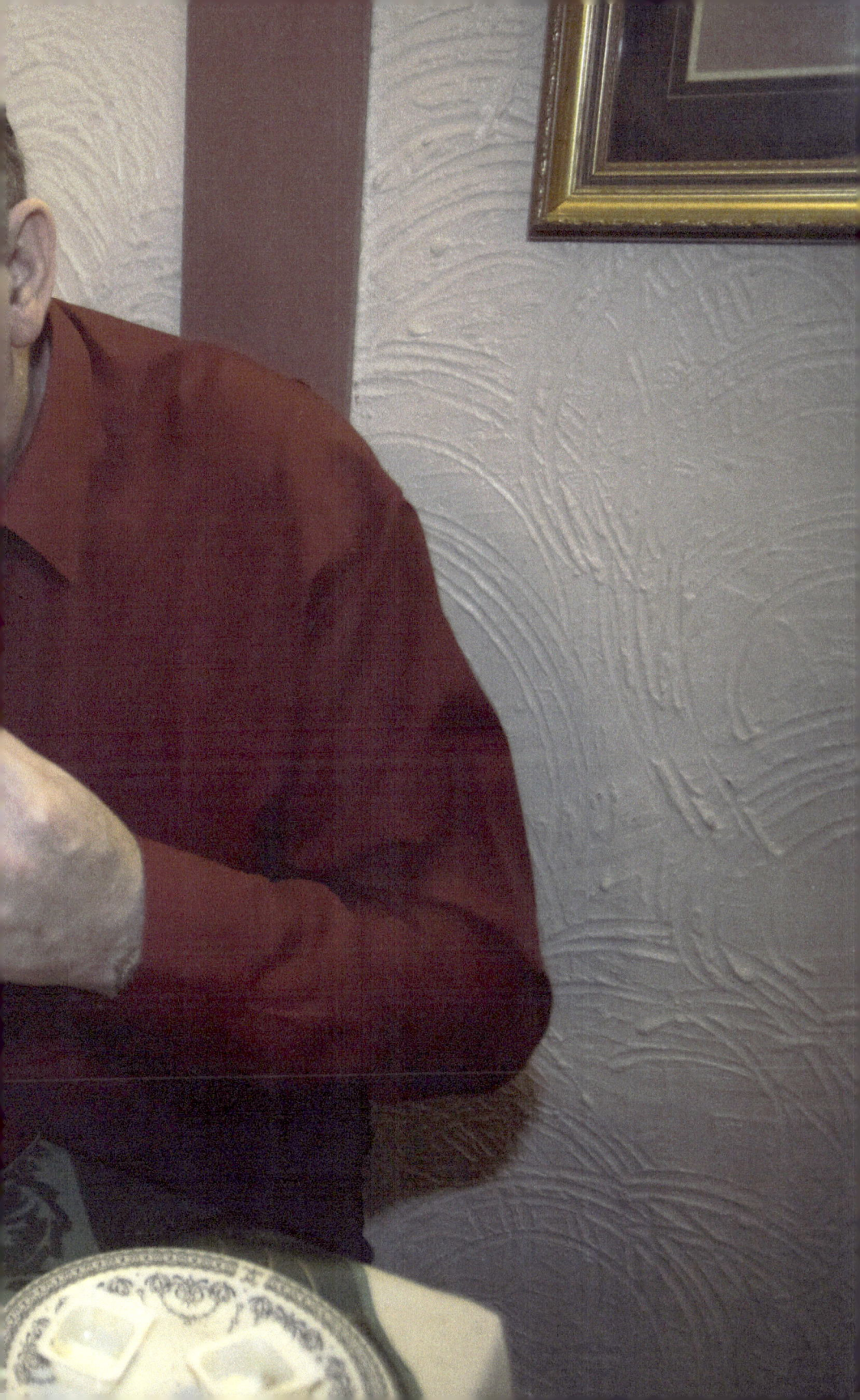

www.ingramcontent.com/pod-product-compliance
Lightning Source LLC
Chambersburg PA
CBHW040846180526
45159CB00001B/332